THE BEDFORD SERIES IN HISTORY AND CULTURE

Reconstruction Violence and the Ku Klux Klan Hearings

D0145627

THE BEDFORD SERIES IN HISTORY AND CULTURE

Reconstruction Violence and the Ku Klux Klan Hearings

Edited with an Introduction by

Shawn Leigh Alexander

University of Kansas

BEDFORD / ST. MARTIN'S   Boston ◆ New York

For Bedford/St. Martin's

Vice President, Editorial, Macmillan Higher Education Humanities: Edwin Hill
Senior Executive Editor for History and Technology: William J. Lombardo
Director of Development for History: Jane Knetzger
Developmental Editor: Danielle Slevens
Editorial Assistant: Arrin Kaplan
Assistant Production Editor: Lidia MacDonald-Carr
Production Associate: Victoria Anzalone
Executive Marketing Manager: Sandra McGuire
Project Management: Books By Design, Inc.
Director of Rights and Permissions: Hilary Newman
Senior Art Director: Anna Palchik
Text Design: Claire Seng-Niemoeller
Cover Design: William Boardman
Cover Art: "Visit of the Ku-Klux," illustration in *Harper's Weekly,* February 24, 1872,
   by Frank Bellew. © Culver Pictures/The Art Archive at Art Resource, N.Y.
Composition: Achorn International, Inc.
Printing and Binding: RR Donnelley and Sons

0   9   8   7   6   5
f   e   d   c   b   a

For information, write: Bedford/St. Martin's, 75 Arlington Street, Boston, MA 02116
   (617-399-4000)

ISBN 978-0-312-67695-7

Foreword

The Bedford Series in History and Culture is designed so that readers can study the past as historians do.

The historian's first task is finding the evidence. Documents, letters, memoirs, interviews, pictures, movies, novels, or poems can provide facts and clues. Then the historian questions and compares the sources. There is more to do than in a courtroom, for hearsay evidence is welcome, and the historian is usually looking for answers beyond act and motive. Different views of an event may be as important as a single verdict. How a story is told may yield as much information as what it says.

Along the way the historian seeks help from other historians and perhaps from specialists in other disciplines. Finally, it is time to write, to decide on an interpretation and how to arrange the evidence for readers.

Each book in this series contains an important historical document or group of documents, each document a witness from the past and open to interpretation in different ways. The documents are combined with some element of historical narrative—an introduction or a biographical essay, for example—that provides students with an analysis of the primary source material and important background information about the world in which it was produced.

Each book in the series focuses on a specific topic within a specific historical period. Each provides a basis for lively thought and discussion about several aspects of the topic and the historian's role. Each is short enough (and inexpensive enough) to be a reasonable one-week assignment in a college course. Whether as classroom or personal reading, each book in the series provides firsthand experience of the challenge—and fun—of discovering, recreating, and interpreting the past.

Lynn Hunt
David W. Blight
Bonnie G. Smith
Natalie Zemon Davis

Preface

Reconstruction was a vital episode in American history. As the nation wrestled over racial justice, political democracy, and the very meaning of freedom, it experienced profound changes and dislocations in its social and political institutions. The story of Reconstruction is taught in every American history or African American history class in the United States, but it is often told with the nation's capital at center stage — that is, from the halls of Congress and the office of the president. This traditional history of Reconstruction leaves out the truth of what was happening on the ground throughout the South. In that troubled region, individuals and groups used violence and intimidation against freedpeople and their white Republican allies to challenge the federal government's plans and restore the South to a condition as close to slavery as possible.

There is, perhaps, no better way to illuminate this aspect of Reconstruction than by examining first-person testimony culled from the 1871–1872 congressional investigation of racial violence in the South, popularly known as the Ku Klux Klan hearings. While the sheer amount of testimony can be overwhelming, this volume presents instructors and students with a representative collection of eyewitness accounts that have been carefully selected and excerpted for use in survey courses. These accounts augment the traditional story of Reconstruction and introduce students to a sampling of African Americans who struggled to survive and prosper in the post-emancipation South. In their attempts to define freedom, obtain an education, advance economically, and simply exercise their constitutional rights, black southerners dealt with the unremitting threat of beatings, sexual assault, and even murder. Also included in this volume is testimony from white vigilantes and their apologists, as well as supporting documents illustrating the battles taking place in the courts and in the press.

Part one situates this rich primary material in the political and social context of Reconstruction. Using the testimony as a foundation on which to build, the introduction explores the major events of Reconstruction, the development and rise of the Ku Klux Klan and kindred groups, the nature and character of the violence that characterized the era, and the fundamental role of this violence in Reconstruction's evolution and eventual downfall. After reading the introduction, students will be prepared to analyze the testimony as historical evidence and consider how it alters or augments the traditional narrative of Reconstruction.

Each primary source document in part two is preceded by a headnote, which serves to provide background, contextualize the document's main themes, and encourage a critical reading. The chronology will help students place the documents and surrounding events in the proper sequence, a list of thought-provoking questions can be used to stimulate class discussion and critical thought, and the selected bibliography will guide students toward resources for further exploration.

ACKNOWLEDGMENTS

This volume, like so many scholarly endeavors, has taken many years to complete and has benefited from the support of a number of individuals and institutions. My work on the hearings began at the University of Massachusetts Amherst while I was researching the writings and intellectual thought of T. Thomas Fortune. It is through the work of Fortune and discussions with John H. Bracey and Ernest Allen Jr. that I discovered the centrality of the congressional hearings to understanding the complicated period of Reconstruction. At Yale University, as a Cassius Marcellus Clay Postdoctoral Fellow, I continued my research into the hearings with discussions with David W. Blight, who urged me to write this volume. At the University of Kansas, I received support from a General Research Fund grant to begin the actual research and writing phases of this book.

So many scholars have generously contributed their thoughts and findings that it is impossible to name them all. I am grateful to David W. Blight, John Bracey, Ernest Allen, Manisha Sinha, Jonathan Earle, Jeffrey Moran, David Goldberg, Clarence Lang, Randal Jelks, Jacob Dorman, Brent Steele, Dave Tell, and Ludwin Molina for their comments, critical advice, and willingness to listen to the details of a gruesome story that needs to be told. John David Smith deserves special mention, not only for his support and guidance but also for helping with a document at a crucial juncture. For their thoughtful suggestions, special thanks go to reviewers Leslie Brown, Williams College; Nicole Etcheson, Ball State University; Jeff Forret, Lamar University; Andrew Kersten, University of Wisconsin–Green Bay; Scott Nelson, College of William and Mary; David Roediger, University of Illinois at Urbana-Champaign; Elizabeth Hayes Turner, University of North Texas; and one reviewer who wishes to remain anonymous. This volume is much better for all of their suggestions and contributions.

My editor, Danielle Slevens, had an amazing ability to pay attention to the details of these rich sources while focusing on major themes. I would also like to thank Mary Dougherty, William Lombardo, Jane Knetzger, Beth Welch, Heidi Hood, Laura Kintz, Arrin Kaplan, Lidia MacDonald-Carr, and the rest of the staff at Bedford/St. Martin's for their patience, encouragement, and assistance. I have worked with many of them on a number of projects over the years, and no publishing group is more professional or enjoyable to work with. Their love for the field and enthusiasm for the work are fantastic and infectious.

I also want to thank T. Thomas Fortune, William Sinclair, W. E. B. Du Bois, and John Hope Franklin, who each in his own way tried to keep the violent history of Reconstruction alive in his writings and reminded us to look for alternative voices in the story. This volume is proof that someone listened, and I hope that it will be used to introduce a new generation of students to the voices of the past and the writings of these towering intellectuals.

Finally, I want to dedicate this book to my family. Leigham and Francis, I thank you for being who you are. I hope that exposing the horrors of yesterday will make your world a little better. Above all else, I deeply thank my best friend and spouse, Kelly Marie Farrell, who has given me love, support, and companionship that I cannot imagine living without. You make my life easy, often without your efforts being fully reciprocated. I thank you for everything you do.

Shawn Leigh Alexander

Contents

Ku Klux Klan: Members, Apologists, Makeup, and Character

Committee Conclusions

APPENDIXES

Introduction: Investigating Violence—White Supremacy and the Rise and Fall of Reconstruction

Rebellion, at least, is honest, in so far that it makes war in broad daylight against organized forces, while, on the contrary, those dastardly gangs direct their attacks against single, defenseless individuals, and surprise, torture, and assassinate them in disguise and under the cover of night.
—*Frederick Douglass*, New National Era, *March 16, 1871*

During the long decade after the Civil War, a period known as Reconstruction, Americans fought over the country's political, social, and moral future. The focus of this debate was the position and status of blacks in post-emancipation America: the meaning of freedom for former slaves and the nature of the redesigned political, social, and economic order in the former Confederacy. In the years following the war, freedpeople asserted themselves as citizens and gained some economic autonomy, basic education, and social independence. In doing so, they defied previous ideas about and meanings of race and challenged the core social and political identities in southern society.

For most white southerners, this new world was intolerable. As historian, sociologist, and activist W. E. B. Du Bois explained in 1935, "When Congress intervened by its reconstruction measures to defeat the reactionary program of the South there swept over that section a

1

crime-storm of devastating fury. Lawlessness and violence filled the land, and terror stalked abroad by day, and it burned and murdered by night."[1] White southerners' rage inspired acts of violence targeting the emblems of the new order: black schools, churches, and homes, as well as teachers, students, white and black politicians, and the freedmen and their families who had gained limited economic autonomy. These acts of violence—politics by the shotgun, whip, flame, and terror—were often led by organizations such as the Ku Klux Klan, a vigilante group founded in Tennessee in 1866, and resulted in the deaths of thousands of African American men, women, and children, as well as hundreds of white supporters, throughout the South.

What is often left out of the discussion of Reconstruction is a true and complete account of this violence. Too often the story of this era is told from the halls of the federal government, with only passing mention of what was happening on the ground in the southern states. If students and scholars want to know the truth about this time period in the South, they must study the testimony of blacks and their white allies. It is in these firsthand accounts that one can see the violence that characterized the various attempts to reunite and restructure the country after the Civil War.

In 1871, amid concerns of infringement on blacks' voting rights and organized white lawlessness, Congress authorized an investigation into the problem of racial violence in the South. The result was an abundance of eyewitness accounts from blacks and whites of many different occupations and persuasions.[2] This testimony provides the most complete and reliable account of what the transition from bondage to freedom was truly like and how widespread vigilante violence was during Reconstruction.

PRESIDENTIAL RECONSTRUCTION AND THE ROOTS OF WHITE VIOLENCE

After the Emancipation Proclamation (1863), President Abraham Lincoln and congressional Republicans agreed that the abolishment of slavery had to be a condition for the return of the South to the Union. In his second inaugural address, a month before his death, the president outlined the task for the nation: "With malice toward none; with charity for all; with firmness in the right, . . . let us strive on to finish the work we are in: to bind up the nation's wounds; to care for him who shall have borne the battle, and for his widow and orphan, to do all which may achieve and cherish a just and lasting peace among ourselves, and with all nations."[3]

While the Civil War still raged, Lincoln attempted to lay the groundwork for rebuilding the nation based on these principles. He sought to restore civil government as quickly as possible to Union army–occupied portions of the South. In December 1863, he issued the Proclamation of Amnesty and Reconstruction, often called the Ten Percent Plan, which promised full pardon and restoration of rights to those who swore loyalty to the Union and accepted the abolition of slavery. Only high-ranking Confederate military and legislative leaders were not eligible. Once those who had taken the oath in a state amounted to 10 percent of the number of votes cast by that state in the 1860 presidential election, the pardoned voters were to write a new state constitution abolishing slavery, elect state officials, and resume self-government. Under Lincoln's plan, new state governments were established in West Virginia, Maryland, and Missouri during 1864 and 1865.

These new governments, despite extending freedom to blacks, denied them full citizenship rights, including the right to vote. Radical congressional Republicans complained. This faction of the Republican party, led by Pennsylvania representative Thaddeus Stevens and Massachusetts senator Charles Sumner, had pressed for more aggressive military campaigns during the war and a quicker end to slavery. After the war, they believed it was essential to democratize the South, establish public education, and ensure the rights of African Americans. They supported black suffrage, often championed land confiscation and redistribution, and were willing to exclude the South from the Union for years, if necessary, to achieve their goals.[4]

Pushing for a stronger approach to Reconstruction, the Radicals proposed the Wade-Davis bill in the summer of 1864, while the nation was still embroiled in war. The legislation, named after its sponsors, Senator Benjamin Wade of Ohio and Representative Henry W. Davis of Maryland, required a majority of white male southerners to pledge support for the Union before Reconstruction could commence in any state and guaranteed equality before the law, though not suffrage, for blacks. The bill passed Congress, but Lincoln pushed back against his Radical colleagues by refusing to sign it into law. Instead, he urged patience with his plan.[5]

After Lincoln's assassination in April 1865, his successor, Andrew Johnson, gave even less consideration to African Americans. Johnson, a Tennessean and former slaveowner, hoped to unify the white South against northern whites and free blacks alike. In May, Johnson outlined

his plan for the reunification of the country. Issuing a series of proc-
lamations, he initiated what is known as Presidential Reconstruction
(1865–1867). Johnson restored all political and property rights, except
the right to own slaves, to southern whites. In addition, he offered pardons to nearly all white southerners who took an oath of allegiance to
the Union. Initially, he excluded Confederate leaders and wealthy planters—those with property valued at more than $20,000—but later he
provided numerous individual exemptions and pardons that brought
these southerners into the fold as well. By 1867, the president had pardoned over seven thousand high-ranking Confederates and property
holders.[6] Johnson also granted the new southern governments a free
hand in managing local affairs. Beginning in late summer 1865, southerners met in state conventions and adopted new constitutions; all, with
the exception of Texas, regained their place in the Union. These states
upheld the abolishment of slavery, but they also maintained loyalty to
the "Lost Cause"—as some southerners longingly termed the defeated
Confederacy—and to white supremacy. Johnson's Reconstruction program, and his lack of interest in protecting the rights of freedpeople,
angered Radical Republicans further.

In 1865, the Thirteenth Amendment officially abolished slavery and
all other forms of involuntary servitude. As Democrats took power
throughout the South, southern legislators began to plan and enact laws
designed to return the region to a condition as close to slavery as possible. Beginning in 1865 and 1866 in Mississippi and South Carolina,
southern states enacted a number of new laws called Black Codes (Document 1). On many levels, these codes, designed to undermine Presidential Reconstruction, were revised versions of the old slave codes.
They sought to define the status of freedpeople and to control their labor,
mobility, and actions. Black Codes were backed up by violence, threats,
or economic reprisals, such as dismissing black farmworkers who tried
to vote or encouraged others to do so.[7] President Johnson took no real
steps to stop this encroachment on the rights of freedpeople, which was
presumably in response to the passage of the Thirteenth Amendment.

Black Codes forced former slaves to carry passes and observe curfews, and they forced many trapped in agricultural work to live in housing provided by landowners. They regulated blacks' rights to marry
and their ability to own and acquire property, gain access to the judicial
system, and negotiate labor contracts. The codes also restricted freedpeople's occupational opportunities, not only by banning African Americans from certain occupations and limiting their options for economic
development, but also by including such legal limitations as vagrancy

laws that allowed a person to be arrested for, among other things, being idle or disorderly or using his or her earnings for things deemed inappropriate, such as gambling. If an individual was found guilty of violating a Black Code, he or she could be heavily fined, imprisoned, or forced into involuntary labor.

Finally, Black Codes gave everyday whites an extraordinary measure of authority over blacks, permitting any white to arrest any black, authorizing the removal of black children from poor families, and allowing white supervisors to whip black workers as a disciplinary measure.

From the start, Reconstruction encountered the violent resistance of white southerners—including both violence that was legally sanctioned by Black Codes and violence that was of a vigilante nature. Southern whites often used terrorism to coerce freedpeople into accepting a subordinate status. This activity became closely associated with the Ku Klux Klan, a secret organization founded in Tennessee in 1866.[8] Soon after its formation, the Klan developed a political agenda, acting as a military arm of the Democratic party and those who wanted the restoration of white supremacy.

Klansmen sought to destroy the Republican party's southern infrastructure, undermine Reconstruction efforts in the various states, restore control over African American workers, and reestablish racial subordination in every aspect of life in the South. They used violence and intimidation to prevent African Americans and their allies from organizing politically, voting, building and operating churches and schools, and engaging in any other citizenship activities. Klansmen whipped, beat, raped, and murdered blacks and their white supporters, often targeting locally influential people such as preachers, teachers, legislators, and law enforcement officials. While most Klan members were small-scale farmers and workingmen, Klan leaders were often prominent members of the community, including wealthy merchants, newspaper editors, politicians, attorneys, and other seemingly respectable citizens. While most white southerners did not participate in Klan activities or other criminal behavior, a significant percentage ignored or explained away the vigilante violence that swept the region.

Although the South was justifiably notorious for its racial violence, opposition to the new order was not limited to that region. Northern whites also found ways to attempt to keep blacks "in their place," whether through laws, local traditions, or acts of vigilante violence. African Americans' access to the vote was limited in the North as well as the South, and blacks throughout the North were also segregated and discriminated against in various public arenas, including hotel accommodations, bars, restaurants, trolleys, and schools.[9] Additionally, immediately after the introduction of the Thirteenth Amendment, white-on-black violence intensified in the North. On the evening of Lincoln's assassination, an Ohio mob torched the main building of Wilberforce University, a historically black college. The fire destroyed all of abolitionist, writer, and prominent black physician Martin Delany's correspondence, manuscripts, and African art collections, which were housed in the school's library.[10]

As southern legislatures passed Black Codes and southern whites regained economic and political power, and as violent resistance to Reconstruction took root in both the North and the South, African Americans began pushing back and demanding their citizenship rights. They used the press — both white newspapers and the rapidly growing black weeklies and monthlies — and held mass meetings to articulate their position. Meanwhile, the Republican majority in Congress stymied President Johnson's Reconstruction plan. In 1865, after returning from a recess, the House and the Senate considered the credentials of the newly elected southern members and decided not to admit them. Instead, they bluntly challenged the president's authority and established a joint committee to study and investigate a new direction for Reconstruction.

RADICAL RECONSTRUCTION, ORGANIZED LAWLESSNESS, AND CONGRESSIONAL INVESTIGATION

While violence against African Americans occurred from the first days of Reconstruction, it became more organized and purposeful after 1867, with the advent of Radical (or Congressional) Reconstruction — the second phase of Reconstruction, in which Radical Republicans took the lead — and the passage of the Fourteenth Amendment, which affirmed African Americans' citizenship and prohibited states from abridging blacks' constitutional "privileges and immunities." Beginning in early 1866, Congress took a series of steps that culminated in its assuming control of the Reconstruction effort. In early 1867, it passed three new Reconstruction Acts. The first divided the South into five military districts and called for sending federal troops to the region to maintain order and protect freedpeople. The second required former Confederate states to draft new state constitutions guaranteeing black male suffrage. The third stipulated that a former Confederate state could send representatives and senators to Washington only after it had ratified the

Fourteenth Amendment, which had been passed by Congress in 1866.[11] All of these laws were enacted over the president's veto.

In 1868, Ulysses S. Grant, a Republican and a supporter of Congressional Reconstruction, was elected president. Although he endorsed Congress's Reconstruction plan and the expansion of black suffrage, restrictions on black rights continued to grow during his two terms. While Grant at times called on federal troops to stop the violence or enforce the laws, he never imposed complete military occupation of the South. Even as the Fourteenth Amendment, ratified in July 1868, conferred citizenship rights on African Americans, the franchise remained uncertain for many black males in both the North and the South.

During Grant's presidency, northern commitment to Reconstruction began to wane, making conditions ripe for the explosion of violence in the South. The old Radical Republicans began disappearing from the scene—Thaddeus Stevens died the year Grant was elected—and the commitment to black rights diminished within the party. Many northerners simply believed that their work was done. Now that the former slaves were technically free citizens, they should rely on their own resources. Others believed that the South should be left to solve its own problems without constant interference from Washington.

Without that interference, however, the white backlash toward African Americans and white supporters of black rights continued to grow throughout the South, even after the enactment of the Fifteenth Amendment (1870), a measure that forbade states to deny the right to vote "on account of race, color, or previous condition of servitude." Many southerners, especially the traditional leadership—including Democratic politicians and the business and planter classes—acrimoniously opposed Congressional Reconstruction. They denounced the new southern governments, in which blacks often played an important role, as corrupt and inefficient. The year 1870 saw the election of the first black U.S. senator and congressman, Hiram R. Revels of Mississippi and Joseph H. Rainey of South Carolina, respectively. In 1875, the former slave Blanche Kelso Bruce of Mississippi was also elected to the Senate and became the first black senator to serve a full term. At the core of white southerners' protests was the fact that many simply could not accept the idea of former slaves voting, holding office, owning land, and enjoying equality before the law. In retaliation for Congressional Reconstruction and the passage of the Reconstruction amendments, and in order to restore white supremacy in public life, they believed that Reconstruction itself must be overthrown. To accomplish this, they launched a campaign of violence in an attempt to end Republican rule.

Members of the Ku Klux Klan, cloaked in disguise, terrorized African Americans and their Republican supporters. The Klan, and analogous groups such as the Knights of the White Camelia, White Brotherhood, '76 Association, Invisible Empire, Pale Faces, Council of Safety, Knights of the Black Cross, and Constitutional Union Guard, existed throughout the South but operated with little central control. In many instances, the Klan came to be a general signifier for any vigilante group operating in disguise. (During this period of the Klan's existence, the white robe and pointed white mask were not the formal disguise. There was no standard costume until the twentieth-century incarnation of the Klan.) Their main goals were to restore white supremacy and destroy the Republican party. Attackers intimidated, disarmed, whipped, or killed African Americans as they saw fit. Klansmen often dragged their victims out of their homes to beat, torture, mutilate, or hang them, or even to set them on fire. Freedpeople had little ability to stop or limit these forms of terror.

In 1866, two large-scale acts of violence drew the nation's attention to the precarious situation of blacks in the South. In early May, black Union veterans in Memphis, Tennessee, came to the assistance of an African American male who was being arrested by white police officers. As a result of the intervention, a three-day riot ensued, in which whites, including police, arbitrarily attacked the black community, killing forty-five people. Only three whites died during the violence.[12] Farther down the Mississippi River in New Orleans, in late July, some forty people died, most of them African Americans, in an altercation between police and a largely black pro-suffrage group. These incidents exposed the failures of Presidential Reconstruction: The South was being returned to the former leadership, and southern blacks could count on little or no protection for their lives and well-being.

These two acts of violence stand out, but only for their scale and the high number of casualties. The racial violence that had long plagued the South had become widespread, creating a climate of terror that touched everyone. At this juncture, southern racial violence also became more targeted and systematized. As W. E. B. Du Bois later noted, "A lawlessness which, in 1865–1868, was still spasmodic and episodic, now became organized. . . . Using a technique of mass and midnight murder, the South began widely organized aggression upon the Negroes."[13] Between 1867 and 1876, while southern officials looked the other way, the Klan and its kindred organizations murdered an estimated twenty thousand black people and maimed, wounded, and terrorized a tremendously larger number.

These acts of violence had a great effect on the southern African American population. As a *New York Evening Post* correspondent noted, in the areas of South Carolina with the most terror activity, "hardly a negro man dared to sleep in his home at night. Many of the women and children would leave their homes on the approach of evening. Working in the fields all day, even there frequently harassed by fears of assassination, they sought at night the woods or fields, and there hid until morning."[14]

This campaign of terror drove Republicans to intervene in southern affairs. In 1870 and 1871, Congress passed three Enforcement Acts in response to specific concerns over the violence used to disenfranchise blacks and disrupt elections. The Klan and similar groups beat, murdered, and generally terrorized whites and blacks who voted or were believed to have voted the Radical Republican ticket. In some regions, they rode through black communities shooting into homes at night or left coffins with organizational markings and dire warnings on potential voters' doorsteps. On May 31, 1870, Congress passed an act that made interference with voting rights a federal offense punishable in federal courts (Document 2). Nine months later, on February 28, 1871, Congress passed the second Enforcement Act, which established a procedure for federal supervision of registration and voting. The third act, passed by a special session of Congress two months later, on April 20, 1871, was popularly known as the Ku Klux Klan Act (Document 3). This law strengthened the felony and conspiracy provisions of the 1870 act, authorized the president to use the army to enforce it, and empowered the president to suspend the writ of habeas corpus—a constitutional privilege meant to prevent the illegal detention of prisoners—in areas he declared to be in a state of insurrection.[15]

With these laws, the Grant administration began to crack down on the Klan, but enforcement remained weak and did little to impede the group's activities. States also were reluctant to enforce the laws. One alternative open to them was to call out their militias. Although militias were used to quell the violence in North Carolina, Tennessee, and Texas, many states were hesitant to employ this form of enforcement because of the cost, citizens' general resentment of a standing military force, and the fact that in many locations the militias were largely made up of African Americans. Authorities feared that arming blacks to suppress vigilantism would only generate more racial violence.

In 1871, Congress authorized an investigation into the problem, sending a joint committee of senators and congressmen into the South. From April 1871 to February 1872, members of the committee solicited testimony from public officials, army officers, victims of violence, and, on occasion, Klansmen themselves about the state of affairs and lack of security. The committee consisted of twenty-one members: five

Republicans and two Democrats from the Senate and eight Republicans and six Democrats from the House. Pennsylvania senator John Scott was designated the chairman. Six of the members were from former Confederate states, and three others were from former slaveholding states that had remained in the Union (Missouri, Delaware, and Kentucky). The Democrats argued that the committee's work was politically motivated and that any evidence of violence the hearings might find stemmed from the corrupt Republican politicians in the South and the dysfunctional reconstructed southern governments. Moreover, they expressed concern that the committee's investigation was confined to only a few states.

The investigation of the Joint Select Committee to Inquire into the Condition of Affairs in the Late Insurrectionary States, popularly known as the Ku Klux Klan (or KKK) hearings, yielded thirteen massive volumes of firsthand testimony. This testimony revealed to the country then, and still reveals today, what one Mississippi resident described as a "reign of terror" affecting blacks and whites alike.[16] Witnesses' accounts demonstrate the clear pattern of brutality that accompanied southern whites' determination to punish black leaders, disrupt the Republican party, reestablish control over the black labor force, and restore white supremacy.

The hearings, which constituted one of the largest investigations in American history, began in Washington, D.C., in May and continued in the nation's capital through September, with a monthlong recess. Congress sent a subcommittee to South Carolina in June and July and additional subcommittees to Alabama, Florida, Georgia, Mississippi, North Carolina, and Tennessee in the fall and winter months. Some less concerted efforts were also made to collect evidence from individuals in Arkansas, Louisiana, Texas, and Virginia.[17] All together, these inquiries, concluding in December, with the subcommittees returning to Washington to organize their reports, became a national phenomenon: They were open to the public and intensely followed in the press, with newspapers throughout the country reporting on the hearings (Document 4).

TESTIMONY OF WHITE VIOLENCE AND BLACK RESISTANCE

Individuals from every segment of the southern population appeared before the committee. Many were subpoenaed to testify about Klan activity, while others came forward voluntarily to share their experiences of violence. Governors, congressmen, state legislators, mayors, law enforcement officials, veterans (Union and Confederate), planters, doctors, editors, merchants, artisans, teachers, laborers, and clergymen — black and white, male and female — all told their stories and created a collective historical memory of the racial violence of the period.

Suspected members of the Klan, and former Confederates in general, gave little helpful information about the violence, generally denying membership in the organization or any knowledge of its activities. General James H. Clanton of Alabama, for instance, said that he did not think there had ever been an organization known as the Ku Klux Klan in his state.[18] He explained that while he had heard of attacks on African Americans by men in disguise, he did not believe that any particular organization was responsible. General Nathan Bedford Forrest also denied the existence of the Klan and his involvement as one of its leaders (Document 23).

African American witnesses proved to be more willing sources of specific information. Hundreds of black women and men came forward, at times at great risk of reprisals. Democratic committee members attempted to discredit their testimony, equating the two-dollar-a-day allowance witnesses received with bribery and accusing local Republicans of coaching witnesses. Nevertheless, their testimony offers abundant evidence of the impact of Klan violence in the South.

The stories witnesses provided yield important insights into the nature of the violence — its causes, its effects, and its role in the undoing of progress and the reassertion of white supremacy following Reconstruction. They also give us a better understanding of what it was like to be a victim of such violence or a witness to it. Their testimony reveals the tactics assailants used and the types of individuals who were targeted.

Violence against African American women was a critical element of the terrorization that took place across the South. Sexual violence was rampant. Witness after witness told of the specific terrors that black women experienced at the hands of white men, sometimes in the presence of their husbands. Victims' shame and fear of violent reprisals meant that many or most of these crimes went unreported. Nevertheless, many brave women — such as Hannah Tutson of Florida and Harriet Simril of South Carolina (Documents 7 and 8) — told investigators about their sexual assaults by Klansmen.

Sexual or gendered violence did not always manifest itself in the form of rape; it also took the form of sexual humiliation and molestation. These attacks were meant not only to dehumanize black women but also to shame black men and challenge their masculinity. A group of night riders who went to the Georgia home of Joe Brown forced all the older individuals out of the house, beat them severely, and made Brown's mother-in-law, sister-in-law, wife, and two daughters "lie down and show their nakedness." The insurgents then proceeded to "[jab] them with a stick" and "[play] with their backsides with a piece of fishing pole." The rest of the women were made to strip off their clothes while the men watched and laughed.[19] These assaults were designed to reinforce the idea that white men controlled the sexual dynamics of the South.[20]

Many victims of violence were involved in local politics. Over one-tenth of African American delegates to the 1867–1868 southern state constitutional conventions were attacked, seven fatally. Witnesses before the congressional committee testified that they were targeted because of their political participation, including voting for the "wrong" candidates, encouraging other blacks to vote, or simply standing up for their political beliefs. Willis Johnson was terrorized in South Carolina for encouraging other blacks to vote in the 1870 election (Document 20). Eliphaz Smith, also of South Carolina, was beaten so badly for voting the Radical Republican ticket that he was unable to feed himself for two days.[21] John Childers of Alabama was threatened and intimidated into voting the Democratic ticket in 1870 (Document 10). Another Alabama resident, Betsey Westbrook, told of her husband's murder at the hands of Klansmen who targeted him for his willingness to stand up for his Radical persuasions (Document 11). Jack Dupree, the president of a Republican club in Mississippi, was murdered and disemboweled within sight of his wife, who had just given birth.[22] Political assassinations took place across color and political lines, including the murder of Samuel Fleishman, a Jewish merchant and Republican sympathizer, and Calvin Rogers, an African American who had raised the ire of local white supremacists as an elected constable in Jackson County, Florida.[23] Political violence also went beyond individual attacks and terrorization: A single attack on Alabama Republicans in the town of Eutaw left four blacks dead and fifty-four wounded.[24]

Violence also became a means of restoring the former system of labor control and preventing African Americans from gaining any type of foothold in the post-emancipation economy. Georgian Alfred Richardson told of groups of attackers abducting and whipping black men and women who asserted themselves on the job, including such transgressions as talking back to their white employers or disputing their wages.[25] Black landowners and their white renters became frequent targets. In Florida, Samuel Tutson and his wife, Hannah, were beaten for not vacating their property. The Klan also tore down their home (Documents 7 and 15). Doc Roundtree and his wife, also in Florida, were beaten in front of their four children because, as the Klansmen explained, "they didn't allow damned niggers to live on land of their own."[26] William Coleman from Macon, Mississippi, who owned land and a great deal of livestock, reported to the committee that his attackers claimed he had become too "bold." As they beat him, the Klansmen told him that he would learn, "God damn you, that you are a nigger, and not to be going about like you thought yourself a white man."[27] Coleman told the committee about other, similar attacks in the area, explaining that the Klan sought these people out "because they had land; they had got too big. They say when you get land or a mule, or get hold of a mule or a horse to sit on, they want to kill you out of getting above your business, or to drive you away."[28]

Indeed, many black citizens who had begun to prosper experienced displacement, including Augustus Blair of Alabama, a black landowner who rented to a white tenant and was driven out by Klan attacks on his family (Document 16). This issue is often neglected when examining the violence of the Reconstruction period. Many African American families that had recently been reunited or were growing in the post-emancipation period were forced to move, often from a rural to an urban setting, to escape violence or the threat of violence. As Henry McNeal Turner—the Georgia-based African Methodist Episcopal (AME) bishop who served in the state legislature briefly in 1868 before he and twenty-six other African Americans were expelled from office by racist white legislators—explained at the hearings, rural blacks "leave the country in many instances because they are outraged, because their lives are threatened; they run to the cities as an asylum."[29] Robert Fullerlove of Alabama, who had been terrorized by the Klan, whose own house had been burned down, and whose landowning neighbors had been killed, told the committee in Livingston that despite his economic prosperity, "it isn't worthwhile for me to stay. I am a hard-working man, and I love what I have worked for and earned, but I declare I can't stay with no satisfaction."[30] It was estimated that nearly three hundred African Americans fled Columbia County, Florida, to escape the terror.[31]

Black autonomous institutions, such as churches and schools, became repeated targets of vigilante violence. White southerners attacked these symbols of freedom and the new order to demonstrate their control of the region. For instance, in the fall of 1870, vigilantes attacked and burned the AME Zion church near Tuskegee, Alabama, wounding several parishioners and killing at least two African Americans in the attack. The violence spread in the months leading up to the 1870 election, to the point that, according to witness William Dougherty, nearly every "colored church and school-house in the county was burned up."[32] Caroline Smith of Georgia, who was attacked by Klansmen (Document 5), also discussed the issue of suppression of education with the congressional committee, telling the investigators that the local schoolhouse remained largely empty as a result of Klan threats to potential students.[33] Individuals who did manage to gain some education were singled out for attack: Scipio Eager of Georgia explained that his brother, Washington, was murdered because he "was too big a man": He could "write and read and put it down himself."[34]

Vigilantes also systematically disarmed southern blacks and confiscated their firearms. John H. Wager, an agent of the Freedmen's Bureau (the federal agency created in 1865 to facilitate the transition from slavery to freedom) in Huntsville, Alabama, explained that attackers seized blacks' weapons "to keep the negroes from having arms about them. They would take the guns generally, at one visit, and then if they did not succeed in getting them, the next time they would come they would whip them. They could come until they got their guns. I suppose that the object was to keep the negroes down. They thought they had no right to have guns."[35] Confiscation of weapons could also diminish black autonomy or self-sufficiency, as Henry Kidd explained: "They were going to stop me from hunting."[36] Disarming blacks served as a symbolic assertion of white supremacy that entailed only a limited use of violence. It also helped reassure whites who were thoroughly frightened about the possibility of a black uprising.

Though their efforts often ended in defeat or suppression, blacks both resisted and retaliated against those who terrorized them. In Belmont, Alabama, when a group of African American men descended on the home of a friend whom the Klan had whipped, they fought with the group of whites they found watching his home, wounding one of them. Shortly thereafter, the black men killed one man and wounded two others who were sent to arrest them. When a white posse formed, the black men became a self-defense force, receiving reinforcements and taking refuge in a swamp with the body of the man they had killed, which they refused to hand over despite the posse's demands (Document 21).[37] Edmund Pettus of Selma, Alabama, told of a similar incident of black resistance, when over four hundred African Americans seized a white suspect whom authorities had taken into custody following a series of murders. They beat the man, stabbed him, and dragged him through the streets, then left him for dead when a group of armed blacks arrived to retrieve him (Document 22). Individuals also resisted the attacks of night riders. For instance, Willis Johnson of South Carolina fired on Klansmen who came to his home in June 1871 (Document 20).

African Americans used arson as a weapon in retaliation for Klan violence, burning down buildings and destroying crops and machinery. Incidents of incendiarism occurred throughout the region, as this form of resistance could be employed by an individual or a group and often could be accomplished with little detection.[38] Alexander Wylie of Chester, South Carolina, testified, "There has been more burning done since the war than ever before since the first settlement of the country."[39]

THE OUTCOME OF THE HEARINGS AND THE LEGACY OF RECONSTRUCTION

In the course of the Ku Klux Klan hearings, African American men and women called on the federal government to recognize them as citizens and human beings. Based on the testimony of hundreds of witnesses and armed with the Enforcement Acts, the Grant administration clamped down on the Klan and other vigilante groups. The president sent several companies of federal troops to the most violent regions, but he used his powers sparingly: Only in nine counties of South Carolina, an area where he proclaimed a "condition of lawlessness" in October 1871, did he suspend the writ of habeas corpus. Federal troops occupied the area and made hundreds of arrests.[40]

Thousands of Klansmen in South Carolina and elsewhere throughout the South fled their homes to escape prosecution. To win justice for victims and gain convictions of the accused Klansmen, overworked district attorneys, constricted by limited budgets and, in some instances, opposed by well-trained and well-funded defense attorneys, fought to build their cases. Federal grand juries issued more than 3,000 indictments, and hundreds of defendants pleaded guilty in return for suspended sentences. At the same time, however, the Justice Department dropped charges against nearly 2,000 others in order to clear court dockets. Of those brought to trial, about 600 were convicted and 250 acquitted. Of those convicted, most received light sentences or fines. In the end, only 65 individuals were imprisoned for sentences of up to five years in the Albany, New York, federal penitentiary for their involvement in vigilante violence.[41]

In addition to the relatively limited success of the Ku Klux Klan trials, general support for Reconstruction was declining. After Grant's reelection in 1872 on the slogan "Let Us Have Peace," federal support for Reconstruction began to wane, and southern Democrats continued to gain power throughout the region. Moreover, the violence continued despite the apprehension of most of the Klansmen. Indeed, the bloodiest moment of Reconstruction took place in Colfax, Louisiana, in 1873, a year after the hearings. In this incident, more than fifty members of a black militia were massacred after surrendering to armed whites who had attacked the town. Nearly three hundred African Americans lay dead at the end of the violence that seized the region.[42]

Therefore, even as the federal government quelled the insurgency of southern whites by investigating and legislating, the violence did not disappear. It merely took on different forms, though the purpose remained the same: to impose white supremacy. In 1874, a group of African Americans from Alabama sent a memorial to President Grant telling him about the "secret assassinations, lynchings, intimidation, malicious and frivolous prosecutions and arrests" that still took place around them. The group explained that they understood that the Klan had been dealt with, but while the night riders had "somewhat changed wardrobe" and "tactics," they remained resolved to reverse Reconstruction "by secret war, violence, and terror."[43] By the end of 1875, white Democrats had regained control of all the former Confederate states except Florida, Louisiana, and South Carolina. The following year, the contested presidential election of 1876 brought Republican Rutherford B. Hayes to the White House, redemption to the last three southern states, and the downfall of Radical Reconstruction.

NOTES

[1] W. E. B. Du Bois, *Black Reconstruction: An Essay toward a History of the Part Which Black Folk Played in the Attempt to Reconstruct Democracy in America, 1860–1890* (1935; repr., Millwood, N.Y.: Kraus-Thomson, 1976), 674.

[2] U.S. Congress Joint Select Committee to Inquire into the Condition of Affairs in the Late Insurrectionary States, *Testimony Taken by the Joint Select Committee to Inquire into the Condition of Affairs in the Late Insurrectionary States*, vols. 1–13 (Washington, D.C.: Government Printing Office, 1872) (hereafter cited as *KKK Testimony*).

[3] Abraham Lincoln, *Speeches and Writings, 1859–1865* (New York: Library of America, 1989), 687.

[4] Eric Foner, *Reconstruction: America's Unfinished Revolution, 1863–1877* (New York: Harper & Row, 1988), 60–62, 66.

[5] Ibid., 61–62.

[6] Eric L. McKitrick, *Andrew Johnson and Reconstruction* (New York: Oxford University Press, 1988), 142–52. See also Foner, *Reconstruction*, 176–227.

[7] Foner, *Reconstruction*, 199–208; Leon F. Litwack, *Been in the Storm So Long: The Aftermath of Slavery* (New York: Knopf, 1979), 366–71.

[8] For more on the Ku Klux Klan, see Allen W. Trelease, *White Terror: The Ku Klux Klan Conspiracy and Southern Reconstruction* (Baton Rouge: Louisiana State University Press, 1995); Hannah Rosen, *Terror in the Heart of Freedom: Citizenship, Sexual Violence, and the Meaning of Race in the Postemancipation South* (Chapel Hill: University of North Carolina Press, 2008); and Lou Falkner Williams, *The Great South Carolina Ku Klux Klan Trials, 1871–1872* (Athens: University of Georgia Press, 1996).

[9] For more on African Americans in the North, see Hugh Davis, *We Will Be Satisfied with Nothing Less: The African American Struggle for Equal Rights in the North during Reconstruction* (Ithaca, N.Y.: Cornell University Press, 2011); Heather Cox Richardson, *The Death of Reconstruction: Race, Labor, and Politics in the Post–Civil War North, 1865–1901* (Cambridge, Mass.: Harvard University Press, 2001); and Leslie H. Fishel Jr., "The North and the Negro, 1865–1900" (Ph.D. diss., Harvard University, 1953).

[10] Dorothy Sterling, *The Making of an Afro-American: Martin R. Delany, 1812–1885* (1971; repr., Garden City, N.Y.: Da Capo Press, 1996), 251.

[11] Foner, *Reconstruction*, 251–91.

[12] For more on the Memphis massacre, see Rosen, *Terror in the Heart of Freedom*, 61–83.

[13] Du Bois, *Black Reconstruction*, 674.

[14] Cited in Philip Dray, *Capitol Men: The Epic Story of Reconstruction through the Lives of the First Black Congressmen* (Boston: Houghton Mifflin, 2008), 83.

[15] Foner, *Reconstruction*, 454–59; Trelease, *White Terror*, 385–91.

[16] Timothy Thomas Fortune, *Black and White: Land, Labor, and Politics in the South* (1884; repr., Chicago: Johnson Publishing Co., 1970), 99; *KKK Testimony*, 12:1029.

[17] *KKK Testimony*, 1:2. See also Trelease, *White Terror*, 392–93.

[18] *KKK Testimony*, 8:229.

[19] *KKK Testimony*, 6:386.

[20] For more information about sexualized violence during Reconstruction and black women's resistance, see Rosen, *Terror in the Heart of Freedom*; Kidada E. Williams, *They Left Great Marks on Me: African American Testimonies of Racial Violence from Emancipation to World War I* (New York: New York University Press, 2012); Laura F. Edwards, "Sexual Violence, Gender, Reconstruction, and the Extension of Patriarchy in Granville County, North Carolina," *North Carolina Historical Review* 68 (1991): 237–60; Laura F. Edwards, *Gendered Strife and Confusion: The Political Culture of Reconstruction* (Urbana-Champaign: University of Illinois Press, 1997); Carole Emberton, "Testimony before the Joint Committee on Reconstruction Atrocities in the South against Blacks," in *Milestone Documents in African American History* (Dallas: Schlager, 2010), 633–49; Carole Emberton, *Beyond Redemption: Race, Violence, and the American South after the Civil War* (Chicago: University of Chicago Press, 2013); and Catherine Clinton, "Bloody Terrain: Freedwomen, Sexuality, and Violence during Reconstruction," *Georgia Historical Quarterly* 76 (1992): 313–32.

[21] *KKK Testimony*, 4:701–2.

[22] *KKK Testimony*, 11:270, 360, 435, 809. See also Foner, *Reconstruction*, 426.

[23] *KKK Testimony*, 13:190, 192. See also Foner, *Reconstruction*, 431; Daniel R. Weinfeld, "Samuel Fleishman: Tragedy in Reconstruction-Era Florida," *Southern Jewish History* 8 (2005): 31–76; and Ralph L. Peek, "Lawlessness in Florida, 1868–1871," *Florida Historical Quarterly* 40 (1961): 164–85.

[24] *KKK Testimony*, 13:222.

[25] *KKK Testimony*, 6:12.

[26] *KKK Testimony*, 13:279.

[27] *KKK Testimony*, 11:483.

[28] Ibid., 484.

[29] *KKK Testimony*, 7:1040.

[30] *KKK Testimony*, 10:1656.

[31] *KKK Testimony*, 13:260–67. See also Trelease, *White Terror*, 310.

[32] *KKK Testimony*, 9:1025.

[33] *KKK Testimony*, 6:402.

[34] *KKK Testimony*, 7:669.

[35] *KKK Testimony*, 9:935.

[36] Ibid., 868.

[37] *KKK Testimony*, 10:1666–67. See also Arnold H. Taylor, *Travail and Triumph: Black Life and Culture in the South since the Civil War* (Westport, Conn.: Greenwood Press, 1976), 26–27.

[38] *KKK Testimony*, 5:1427–28.

[39] *KKK Testimony*, 1:563.

[40] Foner, *Reconstruction*, 457–58; Trelease, *White Terror*, 379–418. For more information on South Carolina specifically, see Williams, *The Great South Carolina Ku Klux Klan Trials*.

[41] Foner, *Reconstruction*, 457–58; Trelease, *White Terror*, 379–418.

[42] LeeAnna Keith, *The Colfax Massacre: The Untold Story of Black Power, White Terror, and the Death of Reconstruction* (New York: Oxford University Press, 2008); Joel M. Sipress, "From the Barrel of a Gun: The Politics of Murder in Grant Parish," *Louisiana History* 42, no. 3 (2001): 303; Ted Tunnell, *Crucible of Reconstruction: War, Radicalism, and Race in Louisiana, 1862–1877* (Baton Rouge: Louisiana State University Press, 1984), 173–209; Foner, *Reconstruction*, 437.

[43] Herbert Aptheker, ed., *A Documentary History of the Negro People in the United States* (New York: Citadel Press, 1969), 600–604.

PART TWO

The Documents

1

Background and Beginnings

1

Laws of the State of Mississippi
1865

Nearly immediately after the Civil War, many southern states began to pass laws—the so-called Black Codes—that were designed to regulate the economic and social conditions of African Americans in the post-emancipation South. These codes required freedpeople to carry passes, observe curfews, and live in designated housing. Stiff vagrancy laws and restrictive labor contracts bound supposedly free laborers to plantations or other industries, and state-supported schools and orphanages excluded blacks entirely. Black Codes as a whole intended to return African Americans to a condition of servitude.

An Act to Confer Civil Rights on Freedmen, and for Other Purposes

SECTION 1. *Be it enacted by the Legislature of the State of Mississippi*, That all freedmen, free negroes and mulattoes may sue and be sued, . . . and may acquire personal property . . . , and may dispose of the same, in the same manner, and to the same extent that white persons may: . . . [but no] freedman, free negro or mulatto, [shall be allowed] to rent or lease any lands or tenements, except in incorporated towns or cities in which places the corporate authorities shall control the same. . . .

Laws of the State of Mississippi, passed at a regular session of the Mississippi Legislature, held in the City of Jackson, October, November and December, 1865 (Jackson, Miss.: J. J. Shannon, 1866), 68, 82–93, 165–67.

SEC. 3. . . . All freedmen, free negroes and mulattoes, who do now and have heretofore lived and cohabited together as husband and wife shall be taken and held in law as legally married, and the issue shall be taken and held as legitimate for all purposes. That it shall not be lawful for any freedman, free negro or mulatto to intermarry with any white person; nor for any white person to intermarry with any freedman, free negro or mulatto; and any person who shall so intermarry shall be deemed guilty of felony, and on conviction thereof, shall be confined in the State Penitentiary for life; and those shall be deemed freedmen, free negroes and mulattoes who are of pure negro blood, and those descended from a negro to the third generation inclusive, though one ancestor of each generation may have been a white person.

SEC. 4. . . . Freedmen, free negroes and mulattoes are now by law competent witnesses . . . in civil cases [and criminal cases where they are victims]. . . .

SEC. 6. . . . All contracts for labor made with freedmen, free negroes and mulattoes, for a longer period than one month shall be in writing and in duplicate, attested and read to said freedman, free negro or mulatto, by a beat,[1] city or county officer, or two disinterested white persons of the county in which the labor is to be performed, of which each party shall have one; and said contracts shall be taken and held as entire contracts, and if the laborer shall quit the service of the employer, before expiration of his term of service, without good cause, he shall forfeit his wages for that year, up to the time of quitting.

SEC. 7. . . . Every civil officer shall, and every person may arrest and carry back to his or her legal employer any freedman, free negro or mulatto, who shall have quit the service of his or her employer before the expiration of his or her term of service without good cause, and said officer and person shall be entitled to receive for arresting and carrying back every deserting employee aforesaid, the sum of five dollars. . . .

SEC. 9. . . . If any person shall persuade or attempt to persuade, entice or cause any freedman, free negro or mulatto, to desert from the legal employment of any person, before the expiration of his or her term of service, or shall knowingly employ any such deserting freedman, free negro or mulatto, or shall knowingly give or sell to any such deserting freedman, free negro or mulatto, any food, rayment or other thing, he or she shall be guilty of a misdemeanor. . . .

Approved November 25, 1865.

---

[1]Neighborhood; used for a law official's patrol area.

An Act to Be Entitled "An Act to Regulate the Relation of Master and Apprentice, as Relates to Freedmen, Free Negroes, and Mulattoes["]

SECTION 1. . . . It shall be the duty of all sheriffs, justices of the peace, and other civil officers of the several counties in this State, to report to the probate courts of their respective counties, semi-annually, at the January and July terms of said courts, all freedmen, free negroes and mulattoes, under the age of eighteen, within their respective counties, beats or districts, who are orphans, or whose parent or parents have not the means, or who refuse to provide for and support said minors, and thereupon it shall be the duty of said probate court, to order the clerk of said court to apprentice said minors to some competent and suitable person, on such terms as the court may direct, having a particular care to the interest of said minor: Provided, that the former owner of said minors shall have the preference, when in the opinion of the court, he or she shall be a suitable person for that purpose. . . .

SEC. 3. . . . In the management and control of said apprentices, said master or mistress shall have power to inflict such moderate corporeal chastisement as a father or guardian is allowed to inflict on his or her child or ward at common law: Provided, that in no case shall cruel or inhuman punishment be inflicted. . . .

Approved November 22, 1865.

An Act to Amend the Vagrant Laws of the State

SECTION 1. . . . All rogues and vagabonds, idle and dissipated persons, beggars, jugglers, or persons practicing unlawful games or plays, runaways, common drunkards, common night-walkers, pilferers, lewd, wanton, or lascivious persons, in speech or behavior, common railers[2] and brawlers, persons who neglect their calling or employment, misspend what they earn, or do not provide for the support of themselves or their families, or dependants, and all other idle and disorderly persons, including all who neglect all lawful business, or habitually misspend their time by frequenting houses of ill-fame, gaming-houses or tippling shops, shall be deemed and considered vagrants under the provisions of this act, and on conviction thereof shall be fined not exceeding one hundred dollars, with all accruing costs, and be imprisoned at the discretion of the court not exceeding ten days.

[2]A person who is argumentative or abusive.

Sec. 2. . . . All freedmen, free negroes and mulattoes in this State, over the age of eighteen years, found on the second Monday in January, 1866, or thereafter, with no lawful employment or business, or found unlawfully assembling themselves together either in the day or night time, and all white persons so assembling with freedmen, free negroes or mulattoes, or usually associating with freedmen, free negroes or mulattoes on terms of equality, or living in adultery or fornication with a freedwoman, free negro, or mulatto, shall be deemed vagrants, and on conviction thereof, shall be fined in the sum of not exceeding, in the case of a freedman, free negro or mulatto, fifty dollars, and a white man two hundred dollars, and imprisoned at the discretion of the court, the free negro not exceeding ten days, and the white man not exceeding six months.

Approved November 24, 1865.

An Act to Punish Certain Offences Therein Named, and for Other Purposes

Section 1. . . . No freedman, free negro or mulatto, not in the military service of the United States Government, and not licensed so to do by the board of police of his or her county, shall keep or carry fire-arms of any kind, or any ammunition, dirk [dagger] or bowie knife. . . .

Sec. 2. . . . Any freedman, free negro or mulatto, committing riots, routes,[3] affrays, trespasses, malicious mischief, cruel treatment to animals, seditious speeches, insulting gestures, language or acts, or assaults on any person, disturbance of the peace, exercising the function of a minister of the Gospel, without a license from some regularly organized church, vending spirituous or intoxicating liquors, or committing any other misdemeanor, the punishment of which is not specifically provided for by law, shall, upon conviction thereof, in the county court, be fined, not less than ten dollars, and not more than one hundred dollars, and may be imprisoned, at the discretion of the court, not exceeding thirty days. . . .

Sec. 5. . . . If any freedman, free negro or mulatto, convicted of any of the misdemeanors provided against in this act, shall fail or refuse, for the space of five days after conviction, to pay the fine and costs imposed, such person shall be hired out by the sheriff or other officer, at public outcry, to any white person who will pay said fine and all costs, and take such convict for the shortest time. . . .

Approved November 29, 1865.

[3]Rout; a disreputable group of people, a violent or unlawful mob.

2

First Enforcement Act
May 31, 1870

The three Enforcement Acts adopted in 1870 and 1871 were Congress's collective response to the violence that seized the South after the passage of the Fourteenth and Fifteenth Amendments. The acts were designed to enforce the Fifteenth Amendment, which safeguarded blacks' voting rights. The first act began to develop in Congress even before the amendment was ratified. During this process, the act expanded into a comprehensive civil rights law, imposing financial penalties on those who infringed on qualified individuals' ability to vote. The act also made it a felony for groups such as the Ku Klux Klan to conspire against, impede, or deny individuals the franchise. By reading through the act, we can discern the diverse means white southerners used to negate Reconstruction and the variety of ways in which Congress sought to deal with the obstruction of blacks' citizenship rights.

Chap. CXIV.—An Act to Enforce the Right of Citizens of the United States to Vote in the Several States of This Union, and for Other Purposes

Be it enacted by the Senate and House of Representatives of the United States of America in Congress assembled, That all citizens of the United States who are or shall be otherwise qualified by law to vote at any election by the people in any State, Territory, district, county, city, parish, township, school district, municipality, or other territorial subdivision, shall be entitled and allowed to vote at all such elections, without distinction of race, color, or previous condition of servitude; any constitution, law, custom, usage, or regulation of any State or Territory, or by or under its authority, to the contrary notwithstanding.

SEC. 2. . . . If by or under the authority of the constitution or laws of any State, or the laws of any Territory, any act is or shall be required to be done as a prerequisite or qualification for voting, and by such constitution or laws persons or officers are or shall be charged with the performance of duties in furnishing to citizens an opportunity to perform

U.S. Statutes at Large, 16:140–46.

such prerequisite, or to become qualified to vote, it shall be the duty of every such person and officer to give to all citizens of the United States the same and equal opportunity to perform such prerequisite, and to become qualified to vote without distinction of race, color, or previous condition of servitude. . . .

Sec. 4. . . . If any person, by force, bribery, threats, intimidation, or other unlawful means, shall hinder, delay, prevent, or obstruct, or shall combine and confederate with others to hinder, delay, prevent, or obstruct, any citizen from doing any act required to be done to qualify him to vote or from voting at any election as aforesaid, such person shall for every such offence forfeit and pay the sum of five hundred dollars to the person aggrieved thereby, to be recovered by an action on the case, with full costs, and such allowance for counsel fees as the court shall deem just, and shall also for every such offence be guilty of a misdemeanor, and shall, on conviction thereof, be fined not less than five hundred dollars, or be imprisoned not less than one month and not more than one year, or both, at the discretion of the court.

Sec. 5. . . . If any person shall prevent, hinder, control, or intimidate, or shall attempt to prevent, hinder, control, or intimidate, any person from exercising or in exercising the right of suffrage, to whom the right of suffrage is secured or guaranteed by the fifteenth amendment to the Constitution of the United States, by means of bribery, threats, or threats of depriving such person of employment or occupation, or of ejecting such person from rented house, lands, or other property, or by threats of refusing to renew leases or contracts for labor, or by threats of violence to himself or family, such person so offending shall be deemed guilty of a misdemeanor, and shall, on conviction thereof, be fined not less than five hundred dollars, or be imprisoned not less than one month and not more than one year, or both, at the discretion of the court.

Sec. 6. . . . If two or more persons shall band or conspire together, or go in disguise upon the public highway, or upon the premises of another, with intent to violate any provision of this act, or to injure, oppress, threaten, or intimidate any citizen with intent to prevent or hinder his free exercise and enjoyment of any right or privilege granted or secured to him by the Constitution or laws of the United States, or because of his having exercised the same, such persons shall be held guilty of felony, and, on conviction thereof, shall be fined or imprisoned, or both, at the discretion of the court, — the fine not to exceed five thousand dollars, and the imprisonment not to exceed ten years, — and shall, moreover, be thereafter ineligible to, and disabled from holding, any office or place of honor, profit, or trust created by the Constitution or laws of the United States. . . .

Sec. 8. . . . The district courts of the United States, within their respective districts, shall have, exclusively of the courts of the several States, cognizance of all crimes and offences committed against the provisions of this act. . . .

Sec. 9. . . . The district attorneys, marshals, and deputy marshals of the United States, the commissioners appointed by the circuit and territorial courts of the United States, with powers of arresting, imprisoning, or bailing offenders against the laws of the United States, and every other officer who may be specially empowered by the President of the United States, shall be, and they are hereby, specially authorized and required, at the expense of the United States, to institute proceedings against all and every person who shall violate the provisions of this act, and cause him or them to be arrested and imprisoned, or bailed, as the case may be, for trial before such court of the United States or territorial court as has cognizance of the offense. . . .

Sec. 10. . . . It shall be the duty of all marshals and deputy marshals to obey and execute all warrants and precepts issued under the provisions of this act, when to them directed. . . .

Sec. 11. . . . Any person who shall knowingly and wilfully obstruct, hinder, or prevent any officer or other person charged with the execution of any warrant or process issued under the provisions of this act, or any person or persons lawfully assisting him or them from arresting any person for whose apprehension such warrant or process may have been issued, or shall rescue or attempt to rescue such person from the custody of the officer or other person or persons, or those lawfully assisting as aforesaid, when so arrested pursuant to the authority herein given and declared, or shall aid, abet, or assist any person so arrested as aforesaid, directly or indirectly, to escape from the custody of the officer or other person legally authorized as aforesaid, or shall harbor or conceal any person for whose arrest a warrant or process shall have been issued as aforesaid, so as to prevent his discovery and arrest after notice or knowledge of the fact that a warrant has been issued for the apprehension of such person, shall, for either of said offences, be subject to a fine not exceeding one thousand dollars, or imprisonment not exceeding six months, or both, at the discretion of the court, on conviction before the district or circuit court of the United States for the district or circuit in which said offence may have been committed, or before the proper court of criminal jurisdiction, if committed within any one of the organized Territories of the United States. . . .

SEC. 13. . . . It shall be lawful for the President of the United States to employ such part of the land or naval forces of the United States, or of the militia, as shall be necessary to aid in the execution of judicial process issued under this act. . . .

SEC. 16. . . . All persons within the jurisdiction of the United States shall have the same right in every State and Territory in the United States to make and enforce contracts, to sue, be parties, give evidence, and to the full and equal benefit of all laws and proceedings for the security of person and property as is enjoyed by white citizens, and shall be subject to like punishment, pains, penalties, taxes, licenses, and exactions of every kind, and none other, any law, statute, ordinance, regulation, or custom to the contrary notwithstanding. No tax or charge shall be imposed or enforced by any State upon any person immigrating thereto from a foreign country which is not equally imposed and enforced upon every person immigrating to such State from any other foreign country; and any law of any State in conflict with this provision is hereby declared null and void. . . .

SEC. 19. . . . If at any election for representative or delegate in the Congress of the United States any person shall knowingly personate and vote, or attempt to vote, in the name of any other person, whether living, dead, or fictitious; or vote more than once at the same election for any candidate for the same office; or vote at a place where he may not be lawfully entitled to vote; or vote without having a lawful right to vote; or do any unlawful act to secure a right or an opportunity to vote for himself or any other person; or by force, threat, menace, intimidation, bribery, reward, or offer, or promise thereof, or otherwise unlawfully prevent any qualified voter of any State of the United States of America, or of any Territory thereof, from freely exercising the right of suffrage, or by any such means induce any voter to refuse to exercise such right; or compel or induce by any such means, or otherwise, any officer of an election in any such State or Territory to receive a vote from a person not legally qualified or entitled to vote; or interfere in any manner with any officer of said elections in the discharge of his duties; or by any of such means, or other unlawful means, induce any officer of an election, or officer whose duty it is to ascertain, announce, or declare the result of any such election, or give or make any certificate, document, or evidence in relation thereto, to violate or refuse to comply with his duty, or any law regulating the same; or knowingly and wilfully receive the vote of any person not entitled to vote, or refuse to receive the vote of any person entitled to vote; or aid, counsel, procure, or advise any such voter, person, or officer to do any act hereby made a crime, or to omit to do any duty the omission of which is hereby made a crime, or attempt to do so, every such person shall be deemed guilty of a crime, and shall for such crime be liable to prosecution in any court of the United States of competent jurisdiction, and, on conviction thereof, shall be punished by a fine not exceeding five hundred dollars, or by imprisonment for a term not exceeding three years, or both, in the discretion of the court, and shall pay the costs of prosecution.

Sec. 20. . . . If, at any registration of voters for an election for representative or delegate in the Congress of the United States, any person shall knowingly personate and register, or attempt to register, in the name of any other person, whether living, dead, or fictitious, or fraudulently register, or fraudulently attempt to register, not having a lawful right so to do; or do any unlawful act to secure registration for himself or any other person; or by force, threat, menace, intimidation, bribery, reward, or offer, or promise thereof, or other unlawful means, prevent or hinder any person having a lawful right to register from duly exercising such right; or compel or induce, by any of such means, or other unlawful means, any officer of registration to admit to registration any person not legally entitled thereto, or interfere in any manner with any officer of registration in the discharge of his duties, or by any such means, or other unlawful means, induce any officer of registration to violate or refuse to comply with his duty, or any law regulating the same; or knowingly and wilfully receive the vote of any person not entitled to vote, or refuse to receive the vote of any person entitled to vote, or aid, counsel, procure, or advise any such voter, person, or officer to do any act hereby made a crime, or to omit any act, the omission of which is hereby made a crime, every such person shall be deemed guilty of a crime, and shall be liable to prosecution and punishment therefor, as provided in section nineteen of this act for persons guilty of any of the crimes therein specified. . . .

Sec. 22. . . . Any officer of any election at which any representative or delegate in the Congress of the United States shall be voted for, whether such officer of election be appointed or created by or under any law or authority of the United States, or by or under any State, territorial, district, or municipal law or authority, who shall neglect or refuse to perform any duty in regard to such election required of him by any law of the United States, or of any State or Territory thereof; or violate any duty so imposed, or knowingly do any act thereby unauthorized, with intent to affect any such election, or the result thereof; or fraudulently make any false certificate of the result of such election in regard to such representative or delegate; or withhold, conceal, or destroy any certificate of record so required by law respecting, concerning, or pertaining to the election of any such representative or delegate; or neglect or refuse to make and return the same as so required by law; or aid, counsel, procure, or advise any voter, person, or officer to do any act by this or any of the preceding sections made a crime; or to omit to do any duty the omission of which is by this or any of said sections made a crime, or attempt to do so, shall be deemed guilty of a crime and shall be liable to prosecution and punishment therefor, as provided in the nineteenth section of this act for persons guilty of any of the crimes therein specified. . . .

Approved, May 31, 1870.

3

Third Enforcement (Ku Klux Klan) Act
April 20, 1871

Congress issued the third and final act to enforce the Fifteenth Amendment in April 1871. Popularly known as the Ku Klux Klan Act, it was one of the most extensive laws of the Reconstruction era. The act, particularly the conspiracy section (section 2), for the first time designated certain crimes as offenses punishable under federal law. The infringement on citizens' right to vote, hold office, serve on juries, and enjoy the equal protection of the laws could now lead to federal prosecution. Additionally, the act allowed the president to suspend the writ of habeas corpus—that is, to allow someone to be arrested and held without charge—in areas deemed to be in a state of insurrection.

Chap. XXII.—An Act to Enforce the Provisions of the Fourteenth Amendment to the Constitution of the United States, and for Other Purposes

Be it enacted by the Senate and House of Representatives of the United States of America in Congress assembled, That any person who, under color of any law, statute, ordinance, regulation, custom, or usage of any State, shall subject, or cause to be subjected, any person within the jurisdiction

U.S. Statutes at Large, 17:13–15.

of the United States to the deprivation of any rights, privileges, or immunities secured by the Constitution of the United States, shall, any such law, statute, ordinance, regulation, custom, or usage of the State to the contrary notwithstanding, be liable to the party injured in any action at law, suit in equity, or other proper proceeding for redress; such proceeding to be prosecuted in the several district or circuit courts of the United States, with and subject to the same rights of appeal, review upon error, and other remedies provided in like cases in such courts, under the provisions of the act of the ninth of April, eighteen hundred and sixty-six, entitled "An act to protect all persons in the United States in their civil rights, and to furnish the means of their vindication"; and the other remedial laws of the United States which are in their nature applicable in such cases.

SEC. 2. That if two or more persons within any State or Territory of the United States shall conspire together to overthrow, or to put down, or to destroy by force the government of the United States, or to levy war against the United States, or to oppose by force the authority of the government of the United States, or by force, intimidation, or threat to prevent, hinder, or delay the execution of any law of the United States, or by force to seize, take, or possess any property of the United States contrary to the authority thereof, or by force, intimidation, or threat to prevent any person from accepting or holding any office or trust or place of confidence under the United States, or from discharging the duties thereof, or by force, intimidation, or threat to induce any officer of the United States to leave any State, district, or place where his duties as such officer might lawfully be performed, or to injure him in his person or property on account of his lawful discharge of the duties of his office, or to injure his person while engaged in the lawful discharge of the duties of his office, or to injure his property so as to molest, interrupt, hinder, or impede him in the discharge of his official duty, or by force, intimidation, or threat to deter any party or witness in any court of the United States from attending such court, or from testifying in any matter pending in such court fully, freely, and truthfully, or to injure any such party or witness in his person or property on account of his having so attended or testified, or by force, intimidation, or threat to influence the verdict presentment, or indictment, of any juror or grand juror in any court of the United States, or to injure such juror in his person or property on account of any verdict, presentment, or indictment lawfully assented to by him, or on account of his being or having been such juror, or shall conspire together, or go in disguise upon the public highway or upon the premises of another for the purpose, either directly or indirectly, of depriving any person or any class of persons of the equal protection of the laws, or of equal privileges or immunities under the laws, or for the purpose of preventing or hindering the constituted authorities of any State from giving or securing to all persons within such State the equal protection of the laws, or shall conspire together for the purpose of in any manner impeding, hindering, obstructing, or defeating the due course of justice in any State or Territory, with intent to deny to any citizen of the United States the due and equal protection of the laws, or to injure any person in his person or his property for lawfully enforcing the right of any person or class of persons to the equal protection of the laws, or by force, intimidation, or threat to prevent any citizen of the United States lawfully entitled to vote from giving his support or advocacy in a lawful manner towards or in favor of the election of any lawfully qualified person as an elector of President or Vice-President of the United States, or as a member of the Congress of the United States, or to injure any such citizen in his person or property on account of such support or advocacy, each and every person so offending shall be deemed guilty of a high crime, and, upon conviction thereof in any district or circuit court of the United States or district or supreme court of any Territory of the United States having jurisdiction of similar offences, shall be punished by a fine not less than five hundred nor more than five thousand dollars, or by imprisonment, with or without hard labor, as the court may determine, for a period of not less than six months nor more than six years, as the court may determine, or by both such fine and imprisonment as the court shall determine. And if any one or more persons engaged in any such conspiracy shall do, or cause to be done, any act in furtherance of the object of such conspiracy, whereby any person shall be injured in his person or property, or deprived of having and exercising any right or privilege of a citizen of the United States, the person so injured or deprived of such rights and privileges may have and maintain an action for the recovery of damages occasioned by such injury or deprivation of rights and privileges against any one or more of the persons engaged in such conspiracy, such action to be prosecuted in the proper district or circuit court of the United States, with and subject to the same rights of appeal, review upon error, and other remedies provided in like cases in such courts under the provisions of the act of April ninth, eighteen hundred and sixty-six, entitled "An act to protect all persons in the United States in their civil rights, and to furnish the means of their vindication."

Sec. 3. That in all cases where insurrection, domestic violence, unlawful combinations, or conspiracies in any State shall so obstruct or hinder the execution of the laws thereof, and of the United States, as to deprive any portion or class of the people of such State of any of the rights, privileges, or immunities, or protection, named in the Constitution and secured by this act, and the constituted authorities of such State shall either be unable to protect, or shall, from any cause, fail in or refuse protection of the people in such rights, such facts shall be deemed a denial by such State of the equal protection of the laws to which they are entitled under the Constitution of the United States; and in all such cases, or whenever any such insurrection, violence, unlawful combination, or conspiracy shall oppose or obstruct the laws of the United States or the due execution thereof, or impede or obstruct the due course of justice under the same, it shall be lawful for the President, and it shall be his duty to take such measures, by the employment of the militia or the land and naval forces of the United States, or of either, or by other means, as he may deem necessary for the suppression of such insurrection, domestic violence, or combinations; and any person who shall be arrested under the provisions of this and the preceding section shall be delivered to the marshal of the proper district, to be dealt with according to law.

SEC. 4. That whenever in any State or part of a State the unlawful combinations named in the preceding section of this act shall be organized and armed, and so numerous and powerful as to be able, by violence, to either overthrow or set at defiance the constituted authorities of such State, and of the United States within such State, or when the constituted authorities are in complicity with, or shall connive at the unlawful purposes of, such powerful and armed combinations; and whenever, by reason of either or all of the causes aforesaid, the conviction of such offenders and the preservation of the public safety shall become in such district impracticable, in every such case such combinations shall be deemed a rebellion against the government of the United States, and during the continuance of such rebellion, and within the limits of the district which shall be so under the sway thereof, such limits to be prescribed by proclamation, it shall be lawful for the President of the United States, when in his judgment the public safety shall require it, to suspend the privileges of the writ of habeas corpus, to the end that such rebellion may be overthrown. . . .

SEC. 5. That no person shall be a grand or petit juror in any court of the United States upon any inquiry, hearing, or trial of any suit, proceeding, or prosecution based upon or arising under the provisions of this act who shall, in the judgment of the court, be in complicity with any such combination or conspiracy; and every such juror shall, before entering upon any such inquiry, hearing, or trial, take and subscribe an oath in open court that he has never, directly or indirectly, counselled, advised, or voluntarily aided any such combination or conspiracy. . . .

Sec. 6. That any person or persons, having knowledge that any of the wrongs conspired to be done and mentioned in the second section of this act are about to be committed, and having power to prevent or aid in preventing the same, shall neglect or refuse so to do, and such wrongful act shall be committed, such person or persons shall be liable to the person injured, or his legal representatives, for all damages caused by any such wrongful act which such first-named person or persons by reasonable diligence could have prevented. . . .

Approved, April 20, 1871.

4

Rome (Ga.) Courier

October 24, 1871

The press covered the Ku Klux Klan hearings with great interest. The political leanings of a newspaper often determined its support or disdain for the committee, the witnesses, and the whole process of the investigation. Democratic publications, such as the Rome Courier *in Georgia, attempted to do whatever they could to discredit the investigation.*

Congressional Ku-Klux Committee.—A sub-committee of this iniquitous body is now holding its sessions in Atlanta. Several witnesses have been summoned from this county, and we may look out for rich developments. The Spanish inquisition was not more disgraceful and dangerous than is this rotten concern. Colonel Sawyer[1] has been summoned to appear before the committee, and will leave for Atlanta to-day. They will be very apt to worm all the secrets of the order out of him. "You bet."

[1]Colonel Sawyer was the associate editor of the paper.

Rome (Ga.) Courier, October 24, 1871, in *KKK Testimony*, 7:674.

2

Ku Klux Klan Violence and the Hearings

Gender and Sexual Violence

5

CAROLINE SMITH

Atlanta, Georgia

October 21, 1871

Caroline Smith, a thirty-five-year-old resident of Walton County, Georgia, spoke to the congressional committee in Atlanta about the Klan's visit to her home. The vigilantes, who had come two weeks earlier, claimed that Smith had spoken out of turn to someone. The special warning they give to her regarding her behavior toward white women tells us a great deal about the traditions of deference that vigilantes sought to uphold, particularly with regard to women. Smith moved to Atlanta following the incident.

CAROLINE SMITH (colored) sworn and examined.

 By the CHAIRMAN:

Question. State your age, where you were born, and where you now live.
Answer. I expect I am about thirty-five years old. I was born in Walton County, but raised from three years old up to nine in Gwinnett; I now live in Walton County.
Question. When did you come to Atlanta?

KKK Testimony, 6:400–403.

Answer. I think we have been here over two weeks; I think last Monday was two weeks ago. I left home on Thursday before the second Sunday in October.

Question. What did you leave home for?

Answer. The Ku-Klux came there.

Question. Tell us all about that.

Answer. They came to my house on Thursday night, and took us out and whipped us; that is about all that it was. . . .

Question. How many were there?

Answer. A great many of them, twenty-five or thirty, perhaps more; but ten of them whipped me.

Question. When was that?

Answer. In the night.

Question. At what time?

Answer. Late in the night; I do not know what time. I sat up very late that night, for they had been there once before, and we never laid down early in the night all of us; some of us sat up the better part of the night. I was pretty nigh asleep when I heard them coming. . . .

Question. How many blows did they strike you?

Answer. They hit me fifty; they had so many men, and they hit me so many licks apiece; they all hit me five licks apiece.

Question. With what?

Answer. With hickories. They did not whip me with a stick; they whipped me with a hickory. . . .

Question. What did they tell you they were doing it for?

Answer. Nothing, only one of them said, "I don't want to hear any big talk." The first time they did not say what they did it for; the last time they said, "We don't want to hear any big talk; and don't sass any white ladies."

6

SARAH ANN STURTEVANT

Atlanta, Georgia

October 23, 1871

Sarah Ann Sturtevant of Walton County, Georgia, provided testimony to the committee in Atlanta about the Klan's attack on her and her older brother, Charley Smith. Similar to Caroline Smith (Document 5), who lived in the same county, Sturtevant said the Klan warned her specifically about the importance of knowing her place before white women.

SARAH ANN STURTEVANT (colored) sworn and examined.

By the CHAIRMAN:

Question. State your age, where you were born, and where you now live.
Answer. I expect I am about twenty-five or thirty years old; I was born in Walton County; and I live in that county now.
Question. Are you married?
Answer. No, sir.
Question. At what place are you living?
Answer. I am living on the place where old Mr. Reeves used to live; the same place where Charley Smith lives.
Question. Are there any people in the county called Ku-Klux?
Answer. Yes, sir.
Question. Have you ever seen them?
Answer. Yes, sir; I saw nine at our house at the time they whipped me, my brother, and sister. . . .
Question. What did they do?
Answer. They gave me forty licks with a hickory, and kicked me once in the head, and hit me on the back of the head with a pistol.
Question. What did they do when they first came?
Answer. When they first came into the yard they came to the door, and Charley Smith ran out, and they caught him. They told him to stand, and he told them he would stand. They commenced beating him in

the back with rocks and pistols and kicking him. He inquired what he had done, and they said it was no matter what he had done; that they had been going for him for a long time, and had caught him now, and were going to pay him up. They then commenced beating him with a hickory.

Question. Who is he?

Answer. He is my brother.

Question. Is he older or younger than you?

Answer. He is older—the oldest child mother has got.

Question. How came they to attack you? Just go on and tell us what they did.

Answer. I asked them what they whipped me for, and they said they had not heard I had done anything, but they wanted to give me a little shillala [shillelagh, or cudgel] for fear I would sauce [sass] white women.

Question. Did they whip you over your clothes?

Answer. No, sir; they stripped them off, and fastened them around my waist.

Question. Did they whip you standing up?

Answer. No, sir; they made me sit down on the ground.

Question. What did they whip you with?

Answer. With hickories. One of them had a wagon-whip, and he whipped me with the stag [handle]; he would not whip me with the whip part.

Question. How many of them struck you?

Answer. There were nine of them, and all struck me.

Question. How many licks apiece did they give you?

Answer. They gave me five licks apiece.

Question. How many struck you with the whip?

Answer. Just one. They all had hickories but one. The one that hit me the first lick had a whip, and he hit me once and walked off, and then the others whipped me with a stick all the time.

Question. Did they hurt you much?

Answer. Yes, sir.

Question. Did they break the skin?

Answer. Yes, sir.

Question. What did they do after they got through whipping you?

Answer. They asked us if we were going to watch them. We said, "No." They said they would leave two or three wild men to see if we would watch them.

7

HANNAH TUTSON

Jacksonville, Florida

November 10, 1871

Klansmen often used sexual abuse to assert their power over black women and to terrorize them into accepting white supremacy. In the process of telling their stories before the committee, African American women were able to reshape the meaning of citizenship, black womanhood, and sexual violence—at least temporarily—in post-emancipation America. Hannah Tutson of Clay County, Florida, traveled to Jacksonville to tell the committee about the Klan's attacks on her and her husband, Samuel, who owned their own land. During her testimony, she reported the traumatizing rape that occurred at the hands of one of her attackers, George McCrea.

HANNAH TUTSON (colored) sworn and examined.

By the CHAIRMAN:

Question. State your age, where you were born, and where you now live.
Answer. As near as I can tell I am about forty-two or forty-three years old. I was born in Gadsden, Florida, and I now live in Clay County, near Waldo, on old Number Eleven Pond.
Question. Are you the wife of Samuel Tutson?
Answer. Yes, sir.
Question. Were you at home when he was whipped last spring?
Answer. Yes; sir, I was at home.
Question. Tell us what took place then, what was done, and how it was done.
Answer. When they came to my house that night the dog barked twice, and the old man got up and went out of doors and then came back and lay down; she flew out again, and I got up and went out of doors; I knew the slut barked more than usual, but I could see nothing; I went back into the house, and just as I got into bed five men bulged [barged] right against the door, and it fell right in the middle of

---

KKK Testimony, 13:59–64.

the floor, and they fell down. George McCrea was the first who got up. I had no chimney in the house, but a board floor, and he went where I had left all the children; went circling around toward the children's bed, and I said "Who's that?" The old man had not spoke. George McCrea ran right to me and gathered me by the arm. As I saw him coming, I took up the child—the baby—and held to him. The old man threw his arms round my neck and held on to me. Cabell Winn catched hold of my foot, and then there were so many hold of me I cannot tell who they were. George McCrea and Cabell Winn were the first to take hold of me. He said, "Come in, True-Klux." I started to scream, and George McCrea catched me right by the throat and choked me. I worried around and around, and he catched the little child by the foot and slinged it out of my arms. I screamed again, and he gathered me again. Then there were so many hold of me that they got me out of doors. After they got me out, I looked up and I saw Jim Phillips, George McCrea, and Henry Baxter. I looked ahead of me and they had the old man; and they tore down the fence the same as if you saw people dragging hogs from the butcher-pen. And they went to another corner of the fence and jerked me over, just as if you were jerking a dumb beast. The old man was ahead of me, and I saw Dave Donley stamp on him. I said "Sam, give up; it is not worth while to try to do anything; they will try to kill us here." They said, "O, God damn you, we will kill you." I said, "I will go with you." George McCrea said, "Come right along." I said, "Yes, I am coming; I will come right along." After they carried me about a quarter of a mile from the house—may be a little more; I cannot tell exactly how far it was; it was a good distance from the house—they took me through a path to a field, and down to the lower end of the field. When they got there he said, "Come here, True-Klux." The True-Klux came there and stopped and whispered about as far as from here to this gentleman, [pointing to a member of the committee sitting at the table.] Then he said, "Now, old lady, you pretend to be a good Christian; you had better pray right off." I cast my eye up to the elements and begged God to help me. George McCrea struck me over the head with a pistol, and said, "God damn you, what are you making this fuss for?" I said, "No." He said, "Where is the ropes?" They said they had lost the ropes. Now, I never saw any horses; I did not see any that night. They went off next to my field and came back with a handful of saddle-girths, with the buckles on them. They took and carried me to a pine, just as large as I could get my arms around, and then they tied my hands there. They pulled off all my linen, tore it up so that I did not have a piece of rag on me as big as my hand. They tied me, and I said, "Men, what are you going to do with me?" They said, "God damn you, we will show you; you are living on another man's premises." I said, "No; I am living on my own premises; I gave $150 for it, and Captain Buddington and Mr. Mundy told me to stay here." He said, "God damn you, we will give them the same we are going to give you." I quit talking to them, only as they asked me anything. They tied me to a tree and whipped me for awhile. Then George McCrea would say, "Come here, True-Klux." Then the True-Klux would come, and they would step off about as far as that gentleman and whisper; and then they would say that they would go off to where the saddles were. They would go, and then when they came back they would whip me again. Every time they would go off, George McCrea would act scandalously and ridiculously toward me, and treat me shamefully. When he saw them coming again he would make me get up. He would make me squat down by the pine, and say, "What are you trembling for?" I would say that I was cold, and was afraid that I would freeze. He would get his knees between my legs and say, "God damn you, open your legs." I tell you, men, that he did act ridiculously and shamefully, that same George McCrea. He sat down there and said, "Old lady, if you don't let me have to do with you, I will kill you." I said, "No; do just what you are going to do." He said, "God damn you, I am going to kill you." They whipped me, and went off again to the horses, and got liquor of some kind and poured it on my head, and I smelled it for three weeks, so that it made me sick. They went off and whispered, and then he told them to go to my house and tear it down. He asked me where was my ox. It was in the field, but I would not tell him; I said that my son-in-law had got my cart. He said, "Where is your son-in-law?" I said, "He has gone to Palatka." He said, "Where is your ox?" I would not tell him. He would whisper to them, and tell them to go and get the ox, and to get my things and start them off to-night. He said, "Let's start them right off to-night." They would go and hunt, and then come back. He would make me sit down while they were gone. Understand me, men, while they were gone to hunt for that ox, George McCrea would make me sit down there, and try to have me do with him right there. They came back and whipped me. I said, "Yes, men, if you will stop whipping me, I will give way to you." Gentlemen, you do not know what expressions Cabell Winn made out of his mouth. It was all smutty [covered with soot, or smut] on their faces, only right from the ear down, and their hands were smutty. Some were in their shirt-sleeves, and some had coats on. I had been working with them very nearly three years. You know that when any person gets about half drunk, he cannot alter his voice but what you can tell him. I have been working and washing for them; I had not been two weeks from his mother's house, where I had been washing; I washed there every week. That is the way they did me; they came back and whipped me. George McCrea said, "I came to dispossess you of this place once before." There were four men whipping me at once.

Question. With what?

Answer. With saddle-girths, as I told you; with surcingles [belts] off the saddles. George McCrea said, "We came to dispossess you once before, and you said you did not care if we did whip you." I said, "Stop, men, and let me see." One of them said, "Stop, and let her get her breath." Mr. Winn talked all kind of nasty talk to me. I got so I did not count Mr. Winn more than he counted me. I told Mr. Winn just exactly three weeks before they whipped me that I did not care what they did for me just so I saved my land. Said I, "In the red times,[1] how many times have they took me and turned my clothes over my head and whipped me? I do not care what they do to me now if I can only save my land." He again asked me if I said that, and I said, "Stop; I will see." After a minute I said, "Yes, I did say so." Cabell Winn says, "Yes, you damned bitch, you did say so." I did not tell anybody but Cabell Winn and his daddy, for my husband was gone. The night they came to whip me they did not expect to find the old man there, and when they found he had hold of me as they were carrying me to the door, he says, "Oh, God damn you, are you here?" And the time they were whipping me they said, "Now, listen, God damn you, at that poor old man; you were a God damned old bitch to get the poor old man in this fix; listen at him, you damned old bitch." I would have told this just the way you hear me tell it now before the others, but they stopped me.

Question. How many lashes did they give you in all?

Answer. I cannot tell you, for they whipped me from the crown of my head to the soles of my feet. I was just raw. The blood oozed out through my frock all around my waist, clean through, when I got to Captain Buddington's. After I got away from them that night I ran to my house. My house was torn down. I went in and felt where my bed was. It was along in the middle of the floor. I went to the other corner of the house and felt for my little children. I could not see one, and

[1]Period of extreme bloody violence after the Civil War.

the bed was hoisted up in the corner of the house and hitched there, and is there now. I could not feel my little children and I could not see them. I said, "Lord, my little children are dead." . . .

Question. Did you find your children?

Answer. I did next day at 12 o'clock.

Question. Where were they?

Answer. They were there at my house, where the true-klux had whipped me. Their father lay out to the middle of the night, and my children lay out there too. They said that when they got away from me they went out into the field, and my little daughter said that as the baby cried she would reach out and pick some gooseberries and put them in its little mouth. When she could hear none of them any more she went up into the field to a log heap and staid [stayed] there with her brother and the baby. At daylight the old man came by a little house I had been living in, and which I used to keep some corn and things in, and they had torn it down, and the hogs had been in there eating up what corn and little stuff I had there.

Question. How old were your children?

Answer. One was about five years old, another betwixt nine and ten, and the other was not quite a year old, lacking two months.

Question. That was the one you had in your arms when they jerked it away?

Answer. Yes, sir.

Question. Did the baby get hurt?

Answer. Yes, sir; in one of its hips. When it began to walk one of its hips was very bad, and every time you would stand it up it would scream. But I rubbed it and rubbed it, and it looks like it was outgrowing it now.

Question. How soon did you see your husband?

Answer. Only when I saw my children. He was whipped so bad he could not travel as I did; he staid at home. When I got back there Mr. Chesnut, a white gentleman, had him there, and he and Mr. Chesnut were sitting there talking.

Question. Did you see where he had been whipped?

Answer. Yes, sir; he could not sit up.

Question. Where had he been whipped, on what part of his body?

Answer. All over it; his legs were whipped, more than anywhere else. They did not begin to whip me as they did him. When I came Mr. Chesnut was there, and unfastening my frock, my daughter gave me some linen to put on, and Mr. Chesnut looked at me where I was whipped. I went by Mr. Rohan Wall's and let him look at me once. But they stand to it to-day, until yet, that that land is not mine; they say it is Tire's. Mr. Winn coaxed me and begged me to give it up before they whipped me.

Question. He wanted to make you give up the land?

Answer. Yes, sir; they came there about three weeks before they whipped me to dispossess me of the place. . . . On Friday while I was eating my breakfast, with nobody there but me and my little children, Byrd Sullivan came to my house with Jake Winn and Dave Donley and George McCrea. They went into the field and let down the fence; the old man was gone to the hammock. Old Byrd Sullivan came up to the house and said: "Aunty, these people are devilish people; they are determined to put you off this land. Now, pay good attention to what I say. When you get your hand into a lion's mouth you pull it out just as easy as you can. Pay good attention to me. I would like to see your old man this morning, but he is not at home. You can tell your old man to give it up, or in a month's time, or such a matter, they will come here, and the lot will push him out of doors and let you eat this green grass." I began to cry, and he said, "You will stop this grieving and crying; tell your old man to keep on writing; I know what you paid for this land; you gave cotton for it." I said, "Yes; I gave cotton enough to come to $150." He said, "Tell your old man to keep on writing, and when he gets the papers for his land let him come to me and he will have his land back." I said, "Mr. Ashly, Mr. Rohan and Mr. Swindell told me not to give it up; that if I let anybody else come on the land I could not get it back."

Question. How long had you been living there?

Answer. Nearly three years.

Question. How many crops had you made?

Answer. Two crops.

Question. And this crop would have been the third?

Answer. Yes, sir.

Question. You spoke about some of them "wanting to do with you," as you expressed it.

Answer. Yes, sir.

Question. What one was that?

Answer. George McCrea.

Question. Did you give way to him?

Answer. No, sir; George McCrea acted so bad, and I was stark naked. I tell you, men, he pulled my womb down so that sometimes now I can hardly walk.

8

HARRIET SIMRIL

Columbia, South Carolina
December 19, 1871

Harriet Simril told the congressional committee in Columbia, South Carolina, the details of her attack and rape by three night riders. The Republican party carried York County, where Simril resided, in the 1870 state elections, and in response the Klan began terrorizing the African American community and its allies. The night riders had already come to Simril's home and beaten her husband on another night, trying to force him to vote the Democratic ticket. On the night they returned, he was sleeping in the woods to avoid another attack.

HARRIET SIMRIL (colored) was called as a witness for the prosecution, and, being duly sworn, testified as follows:

Question. Who is your husband?
Answer. Sam Simmons.
Question. Where do you live?
Answer. At Clay Hill, in York county.
Question. How long have you lived there?
Answer. A good many years.
Question. Has your husband lived there a good many years?
Answer. Yes, sir.
Question. Did he vote at the last election?
Answer. Yes, sir.
Question. Do you know what politics he is?
Answer. He is a radical.
Question. Did the Ku-Klux ever visit your house?
Answer. Yes, sir; I think along in the spring.
Question. About what time in the spring?
Answer. I cannot tell you exactly.
Question. Have they been there more than once?
Answer. Yes, sir; they came on him three times.

KKK Testimony, 5:1861–62.

Question. Now tell the jury what they did each time.

Answer. The first time they came my old man was at home. They hollered out "open the door," and he got up and opened the door. They asked him what he had in his hand; he told them the door-pin. They told him to come out, and he came out. These two men that came in, they came in and wanted me to make up a light; the light wasn't made up very good, and they struck matches to a pine stick and looked about to see if they could see anything. They never said anything, and these young men walked up and they took my old man out after so long; and they wanted him to join this democratic ticket; and after that they went a piece above the house and hit him about five cuts with the cowhide.

Question. Do you know whether he promised to be a democrat or not?

Answer. He told them he would rather quit all politics, if that was the way they was going to do to him.

Question. What did they do to you?

Answer. That is the second time they came. They came back after the first time on Sunday night after my old man again, and this second time the crowd was bigger.

Question. Did they call for your old man?

Answer. Yes, sir; they called for him, and I told them he wasn't here; then they argued me down, and told me he was here. I told them no, sir, he wasn't here. They asked me where was my old man? I told them I couldn't tell; when he went away he didn't tell me where he was going. They searched about in the house a long time, and staid with me an hour that time; searched about a long time, and made me make up a light; and after I got the light made up, then they began to search again, and question me again about the old man, and I told them I didn't know where my old man had gone.

Question. What did they do to you?

Answer. Well, they were spitting in my face and throwing dirt in my eyes; and when they made me blind they bursted open my cupboard. I had five pies in my cupboard, and they eat all my pies up, and then took two pieces of meat; then they made me blow up the light again, cursing me; and after awhile they took me out of doors and told me all they wanted was my old man to join the democratic ticket; if he joined the democratic ticket they would have no more to do with him; and after they had got me out of doors, they dragged me into the big road, and they ravished me out there.

Question. How many of them?

Answer. There was three.

Question. One right after the other?

Answer. Yes, sir.

Question. Threw you down on the ground?

Answer. Yes, sir, they throwed me down.

Question. Do you know who the men were who ravished you?

Answer. Yes, sir, can tell who the men were; there were Ches McCollum, Tom McCollum, and this big Jim Harper.

Question. Who ravished you first?

Answer. Tom McCollum grabbed me first by the arm.

Question. What next?

Answer. All nasty talk they put out of their mouths. (Witness here detailed the conversation on the part of her tormentors, but it was of too obscene a nature to permit of publication.)

Question. What was your condition when they left you? How did you feel?

Answer. After they got done with me I had no sense for a long time. I laid there, I don't know how long.

Question. Did you get up that night?

Answer. Yes, sir, and walked back to the house again.

Question. Have the Ku-Klux ever come to you again?

Answer. No, sir; they never came back no more after that; they came back, too, but I was never inside the house.

Question. Did your husband lay out at night?

Answer. Yes, sir; and I did too—took my children, and when it rained thunder and lightning.

Question. When they came back what did they do?

Answer. When they came I wasn't there; I went there the next morning, and there was a burnt chunk down in the corner.

Question. Did it burn the house any?

Answer. No, sir; it didn't burn it—they done that to scare my old man, and after that my old man and me drowned our fire out every night, and went away.

Question. Did they come there any more?

Answer. They didn't come any more, at all; the house was burned the next morning when I went to it.

Question. Did they burn your house down?

Answer. Yes, sir; I don't know who burnt it down, but the next morning I went to my house and it was in ashes.

Question. Why did you lay out?

Answer. We laid out in the woods.

The Court. Why did you lay out?

Answer. We went a way up towards the river.

Question. To get out of the way of the Ku-Klux?

Answer. Yes, sir; I got out of the way of them.

Question. That is what you went for?

Answer. Yes, sir.

Question. How long did you and your old man lay out?

Answer. I think we laid out for four nights. Yes, we lay out four nights; I cannot exactly tell how many nights, but he lay out a long time before I lay out.

Question. Did these Ku-Klux have on masks and gowns?

Answer. Yes, sir; they had on gowns, and they had on false caps on their faces.

(The defense waived cross-examination.)

Political Violence: The Franchise

9

ABRAM COLBY

Atlanta, Georgia

October 27 and 28, 1871

Abram Colby, a former slave whose owner (who was also Colby's father) freed him upon his death, was a Republican member of the Georgia state legislature during Reconstruction. In October 1869, a group of Democrats offered Colby $5,000 to give up his seat to a white Democrat. When he refused the bribe, a group of nearly seventy-five Klansmen dragged him from his house and beat him for almost three hours. Colby also owned a small plantation that the vigilantes refused to allow him to live on free of disruption. As Colby explained to the committee, "I could make as

KKK Testimony, 7:695–707.

comfortable a living there as anywhere in the world if they would leave me alone."

ABRAM COLBY (colored) sworn and examined.

By the CHAIRMAN:

Question. State your age, where you were born, and where you now live.

Answer. I am fifty-two years old. I was born in Greene County and it is my home now when I can live there.

Question. Were you a slave before the war?

Answer. Yes, sir; I was raised by my father, and I was a slave of his.

Question. Were you living with him at the time of the emancipation?

Answer. No, sir; he was dead then. He left me free when he died.

Question. How many years have you been free?

Answer. About twenty years.

Question. What was your occupation before the war?

Answer. I used to be a barber.

Question. Did you take any part in the politics of the country after the war was over and reconstruction had commenced?

Answer. Yes, sir, I did, after the war was over.

Question. What part did you take?

Answer. I took the republican part.

Question. You acted with the republican party?

Answer. Yes, sir.

Question. You took a prominent and active part?

Answer. I think so.

Question. Have you held any office or position?

Answer. I was elected to the legislature.

Question. Which legislature?

Answer. In 1868.

Question. To which house?

Answer. To the lower house.

Question. Were you one of those who were expelled?

Answer. Yes, sir.

Question. And then reinstated?

Answer. Yes, sir.

Question. Are you a member of the next house?

Answer. Yes, sir; I was elected to the next legislature.

Question. Tell us whether at any time you have had any violence offered to you; and if so, tell us what it was.

Answer. On the 29th of October, 1869, they came to my house and broke my door open, took me out of my bed and took me to the woods and whipped me three hours or more and left me in the woods for dead. They said to me, "Do you think you will ever vote another damned radical ticket?" I said, "I will not tell you a lie." They said, "No; don't tell a lie." I thought I would not tell a lie. I supposed they would kill me anyhow. I said, "If there was an election to-morrow, I would vote the radical ticket." They set in and whipped me a thousand licks more, I suppose.

Question. With what did they whip you?

Answer. With sticks and with straps that had buckles on the ends of them.

Question. How many were engaged in that?

Answer. Sixty-five came to my house and took me out; only twenty-five whipped me, so I understood after they thought I was dead. . . .

Question. Was that before you had been expelled from the legislature?

Answer. No, sir; it was after, and before I was seated again.

Question. What is the character of those men who were engaged in whipping you?

Answer. Some of them are the first-class men in our town. One is a law-yer, one a doctor, and some are farmers; but among them some are not worth the bread they eat. I have heard a great many names since, but I did not know them that night.

Question. Did they have any talk with you before they took you out?

Answer. No, sir. They broke my door down. I was asleep. They called out, "Surrender!" I said, "Of course I surrender." They had their pis-tols, and they took me in my night-clothes and carried me a mile and a quarter from home. I may say that they hit me five thousand blows. I told President Grant the same that I tell you now. After they thought I was dead, Doctor Walker came up to feel my pulse. Finding my wrist all wet and bloody, he did not feel my pulse, but said, "He is dead." Tom Robinson was commanding the crowd. Two of them said, "Cap-tain, we have not struck him a lick." He said, "Yes, all of you have." They said, "Only twenty-three of us have whipped him." He said, "Go on and lick him; he is a dead man." One of them came up and struck me. I counted his licks. At that time they did not hurt me a bit, except about the neck. He struck me two hundred licks. They gave me four or five hundred before they commenced counting. They told me to take off my shirt. I said, "I never do that for any man." They tried to knock me down with their sticks, but they could not do it. My draw-ers fell down about my feet, and they took hold of them and pulled them, and tripped me up. They then pulled my shirt up over my head. They said I had voted for Grant, Bullock, and Blodgett.

Question. You had voted in the legislature for Foster Blodgett, and had voted at the polls for Bullock and Grant?

Answer. Yes, sir.

Question. And that was the reason they gave for whipping you?

Answer. Yes, sir; and they said I had influence with the negroes of other counties, and had carried the negroes against them. About two days before they whipped me they offered me $5,000 to turn and go with them, and said they would pay me $2,500 cash if I would turn and let another man go to the legislature in my place. I told them that I would not do it if they would give me all the county was worth; that Foster Blodgett had always been a true man to me and to my party. One of them laughed and said, "You have a son named Foster Blodgett." I said, "Yes, I have." That night when they whipped me they said, "You named a little son of yours Foster Blodgett; we will give you a hundred more for that"; and they did so. The worst thing about the whole matter was this: My mother, wife, and daughter were in the room when they came there and carried me out. My little daughter came out and begged them not to carry me away. They drew up a gun and actually frightened her to death. She never got over it until she died.

Question. How long did she live?

Answer. About a year.

Question. Had she ever been sick before?

Answer. No, sir; that was the part that grieves me the most about the whole thing. I was at my house a week ago, but I staid in the woods that night; they were around there looking for me.

Question. Have you property down there?

Answer. Yes, sir; I have a small plantation, and I could make as comfortable a living there as anywhere in the world if they would leave me alone. I cannot live there.

Question. Have any of those men been punished for this transaction?

Answer. No, sir. I would have come before the court here last week, but I knew it was no use for me to try to get Ku-Klux condemned by Ku-Klux, and I did not come. Mr. Saunders, a member of the grand jury here last week, is the father of one of the very men I knew whipped me. What was the use of my going before that grand jury? Several tried to get me to come, but I said, "I will not go before that court if I never get them punished; for I know that court will never punish them."

Question. Why have you not brought a civil action for damages against them?

Answer. I did not see that I could get anything; that is the reason why I have not done it.

10

JOHN CHILDERS

Livingston, Alabama

November 1, 1871

John Childers, a laborer in Sumter County, Alabama, described to the committee the brutal violence that ran rampant in the county in 1870 and 1871. He described vigilantes' acts of violence against him and the ways in which they used terror to convince him to vote the Democratic ticket. He also shared with the committee the brutal beating of his adolescent daughter, who had forgotten the cap of an infant she was hired to look after.

JOHN CHILDERS (colored) sworn and examined.

By the CHAIRMAN:

Question. Where do you live?

Answer. About a mile and a quarter from here, at Mr. Lee's place.

Question. How long have you lived in Sumter County?

Answer. All my life; forty-two years the 11th of this month.

Question. Can you read and write?

Answer. No, sir.

Question. Do you own any land?

Answer. No, sir.

Question. Whose land do you work?

Answer. I have not worked any person's this year at all, sir. My family is on Mr. Lee's place—a rented place.

Question. Have you ever been maltreated in any way by men at night?

Answer. Yes, sir.

Question. You may state to the committee the circumstances.

Answer. Do you mean by disguised men, or men in their natural?

Question. It makes no difference whether they were disguised or not. State the circumstances.

KKK Testimony, 10:1719–28.

Answer. I was going from this town here; on the bridge, right down here, I was attacked by some men; they rode up to me, struck me over the head with a double-barreled shot-gun. The scars are here on my skull to show for themselves; but what time it was, at this presence, I don't remember.

Question. How long ago was this?

Answer. It was some time last year—in the fall of the year.

Question. How many men were there?

Answer. There were three, I think, in the party; and if it had not been for a brother-in-law of one of the party, I would have been killed.

Question. What did he do to save you?

Answer. He took hold of me and told his brother-in-law that I was a good boy, and it was wrong for him to treat me in that way. . . .

Question. What do you know of any other colored people in this county, besides yourself, being beaten or shot, or in anywise injured by the whites?

Answer. Do you intend for me to tell everything?

Question. Everything you know. Take up one case after another, and let us know all of them.

Answer. Well, gentlemen, I am delicate in expressing myself. I feel myself in great risk in doing these things. I have no support in the State of Alabama. I am a citizen here, bred and born; and have been here forty-two years. If I report these things I can't stay at home.

Question. We will not require you, against your will, to give the names of the men who have done these acts of violence. We simply called you to state what colored people had been whipped, shot, or otherwise maltreated, and if you don't choose to give the names of the men who committed these acts of violence, we will not press you to do it. . . .

Answer. I know one thing of my own; a daughter of mine; not by Ku-Klux; would that be acceptable?

Question. Yes.

Answer. She was awful badly whipped. I was not here. I was in Mississippi. I came here the day after she was whipped. I got back the next day. She lived seven days after I got home. My wife hired her out to a man while I was gone, and he awfully abused her. It was done the Wednesday before the last 4th of July. You can count back from the last 4th of July and see what time it came on.

Question. Was there more than one person concerned in whipping her?

Answer. No, sir; Mr. Jones, who had her employed from my wife, he was the one that did it. I aimed to prosecute him at the last gone [*sic*] court, but the witnesses, by some means or other, was run away. I don't know; I could not tell how they got them out of the way. There was no case made of them.

Question. Did she die because of the whipping?

Answer. I am satisfied that she did. I can't say that, but I am satisfied that she did.

Question. Did you see her body after she had been whipped?

Answer. I did; I examined her myself; I buried her with scars on her that long, [illustrating;] a finger-length.

By Mr. RICE:

Question. How long after the whipping did she die?

Answer. In eight days.

Question. How old was she?

Answer. She would have been ten years old the 26th of next August.

By the CHAIRMAN:

Question. What was she whipped for?

Answer. She was hired out as a nurse to see to the baby; she had taken the baby out in the front yard among a parcel of arbor vitae; and, being out there, the baby and she together, she was neglectful, so as to leave the baby's cap out where it was not in place when the mother of the child called for the cap, and it could not be found. That is what she told me when I came home that she was whipped for. . . . [The witness weeping.]

Question. And then she told you the particulars of how she had been whipped, did she?

Answer. She came up. I had been gone away from here, then, about three months, or a little more. I left them on the 20th of March. I didn't hire her to Mr. Jones myself; my wife did that in my absence. When I came she told me the condition of everything, and how she had been treated by Mr. Jones. Well, I was glad to see my wife and child, and the balance of the children, and didn't pay much attention to her that night. I come on the train that night, and got off the train below here at Hook's Station, and walked through two miles the nigh way home. She was sitting in the door, and I asked her how it come she was not playing with the rest of the children. She says, "Papa, I am so sore I can't play." I says, "What's the matter with you?" She says, "Mr. Jones has beat me nearly to death." I says, "He did?" She says, "Yes." She pulled up her coat here and showed me. "Look here, papa, where he cut me," and there were great gashes on her thighs, as long as my finger. I buried her with them. I charged on her mother then for hiring her to Mr. Jones. She says, "I had them all here and could not tend to them all in your absence; and Mr. Jones told me he would treat my children well if I would let him have them." He had my son and daughter both there; my boy was still with Mr. Jones. He didn't come away. I didn't pay a great deal of attention to her, only to examine and see where she was whipped. The next morning I come here to town. That was Friday night that I came home. She says, "Papa, I want you to get me one of those little roll-combs the little girls roll their hair with." When I got to town I got with my acquaintances and forgot it, and when I got home, Saturday night, she asked me and I told her I didn't have it, but I would get it Monday. I came here Monday, and when I got back she was sick and speechless, and there she lay speechless. From that time till she died she never spoke again. I carried the comb home to her about 12 o'clock Monday. I tried to amuse her and says, "Daughter, here's your comb." She took it in her hand and laid it down by her, like that, [illustrating,] but she never did speak and never has spoken. Tuesday she seemed a little better in the morning than she was Monday, and I went off to John, a neighbor, to plow for him. I thought I would work a few days while I staid here, and she still—Tuesday after I left—kept getting worse. My wife sent for me about dinner-time. I went home and looked at her and felt of her. She still was speechless. I felt of her and she commenced sweating so freely I thought she was getting better. I thought she was sweating off the fever, and will be all right directly, through the course of the evening. She didn't get no better from the sweating of the fever. I suppose it was the change for death; I don't know what it was. Wednesday morning she seemed to be right quiet and peaceable, and laying there not speaking yet, and I went off still to this neighbor's to plow; and about two hours after I got away from home my wife sent for me, and I come and examined her, and set down by the bed and staid there and tried to amuse her, and still she didn't talk none. I commenced examining her then, and stripped up her clothes, and I found bruised places all over her body, up here, you know, [indicating the waist.] I told my wife I thought it a hopeless case. She says, "John, send for the doctor." I says, "No, wait a little while, and see if she don't get better." That was Tuesday. I failed to send for the doctor till Wednesday. I come to town then. She seemed, after daylight, to commence sinking and getting worse. I come to town for the doctor at daylight—Dr. Garber. He went over and examined her, and said: "She has congested the brains, and pour water on her just as long as she would breathe." That was enough to satisfy me she was going to die right away. He said, "pour water on her as long as she would breathe." I said, "I think it is a hopeless case, from what he says. If he thinks there is any hope of her getting well, he wouldn't ask us to pour water on her after she gets over this." He said, "Pour water on her as long as she would breathe." My wife says, "I noticed that." The doctor come and staid with her about three hours, and set right by her, and poured water on her himself. He got on his horse when he got ready to start, and said: "John, pour water on her; I will come back this evening." Between the time he was gone he left some medicine for her to take. I gave her medicine, and I think she got a little better. She took the medicine when I put it in her mouth. She swallowed it freely; and I told the doctor when he came I thought she was getting a little better. He examined her, and said: "Continue to pour water on her just as long as she will breathe." About 7 o'clock in the evening she died — about sundown. I tried to make a case of that; but the witnesses all went off. I think that she died from the abuse, myself — that's my notion about it; but, by some accident or other, the witnesses all went off, and I couldn't make no case out of it myself, because I was not here myself, and didn't see what was done to her.

Question. Has nothing ever been done with Mr. Jones?

Answer. No, sir; nothing at all. He came to me the day before court and asked me for a compromise on the case. Well, I had to compromise, because I had no witnesses. I told him I must give it up. I didn't see nothing that he did to her, and the ones that did see it were gone away.

11

BETSEY WESTBROOK

Demopolis, Alabama

October 24, 1871

Betsey Westbrook, of Jefferson, Alabama, came to the congressional hearings in Demopolis to tell of the murder of her husband, Robin, for his political leanings. The vigilantes who came to their home killed Robin in front of Betsey and her son.

KKK Testimony, 9:1242–47.

BETSEY WESTBROOK (colored) sworn and examined.

By the CHAIRMAN:

Question. Where do you live?

Answer. I have been staying down with Judge O'Connor, but he has moved out, and I am fixing to move myself.

Question. Where did you live before you came here?

Answer. In Jefferson; in the city of Jefferson.

Question. Is that in this county?

Answer. It's about eleven miles from here, down in Jefferson beat.

Question. What was your husband's name?

Answer. Robin Westbrook.

Question. Has he been killed?

Answer. Yes, sir; he was killed.

Question. How long ago?

Answer. He was killed the 18th of July.

Question. Of this present year?

Answer. Yes, sir; this year.

Question. Where was he killed?

Answer. He was killed right in the house, right where I was staying, living with a man named James Norwood.

Question. You may give to the committee the particulars of his being killed.

Answer. Yes, sir.

Question. Go on and state the whole case.

Answer. At the first beginning they came up behind the house that night—the white men came up behind the house.

Question. Did they have disguises on their faces?

Answer. One of them had his face smutted, and another had on a knit cap on his face.

Question. How many of them were there?

Answer. Six men came in the house and one staid at the door, making seven, and there was some standing at the windows.

Question. Were they armed?

Answer. Yes, sir, all were armed; they all had arms with them that I saw.

Question. Pistols?

Answer. Yes, sir. The man that killed my husband had a pistol about that long, [six inches.]

Question. Was this after night?

Answer. Yes, sir, about 11 o'clock at night.

Question. Had you gone to bed?

Answer. I was gone to bed, but he was not.

Question. What did these men say they came for?

Answer. They didn't say. They first came and shot about seven barrels through the window, at the end of the house, at his head. He called Mr. Norwood, and told him somebody was breaking in the house, and Mr. Norwood, after he heard him, came out, and they told him not to come; they didn't wish to hurt him. They told him to open his door. He said he wouldn't for any man at that time.

Question. Who?

Answer. The white man. They said, "You had better open it, it will be better for you." One of them said, "Get a rail and bust the door down." They went to the fence and got a rail and broke down the outside door. We shut ourselves up then in another room in the back of the house, and they got another rail and busted open the back door, and one of them said, "Raise a light." I was sitting on a little basket on the hearth. They picked it up and pitched it in the fire, and it had grease on it, and it blazed up and made a light. Then they saw where they stood, and one of them run in and began to strike him over the head, and says, "You are that damned son of bitch Westbrook?" He says, "Yes, I am." The man struck him with his gun. The man had a gun and run at him and struck him on the head, and his hat fell off of his head. Then my husband took the dog-iron [andiron] up and he struck three or four of them, and the first man he struck he knocked down. They got him jammed up in the corner, and one man went around behind him and put two loads out of a double barreled gun in his shoulders.

Question. Did he go around outside of the house?

Answer. No, sir; but he came around behind him as he was there, and put two loads out of a double barreled gun in his shoulder, and then he dropped the dog-iron down; and another man says, "Kill him, God damn him," and he took a pistol and shot him right down, here in the neck, over the left shoulder. Then he fell right down and hollered. He didn't live more than half an hour after they shot him.

Question. What did they do then?

Answer. After he fell and hollered, then they just all got up and run out. They left that hat lying there, and one of the men came back and got that hat. That was the first man that fell. He dropped down, and they took him out of the house and set him under the chimney back of a tree, and the blood strung across the house, and the fence, and the cotton patch, and in the road.

Question. Did they go away then?

Answer. Yes, sir; but my boy was in there while they were killing my husband, and he says, "Mammy, what must I do?" and I says, "Jump out doors and run." He went to the door and a white man took him by the arm, and says, "G——d d——n you, I will fix you too," but he snatched himself loose and got out of the door, and another one whacked him on the back of the head, but he got away. They shot two loads after him, but he got clear away. If I hadn't made him run they would have killed him too; they were going to kill them both.

Question. Did you know any of these men?

Answer. Yes, sir; I knew the voices of two before they came into the house.

Question. Give their names.

Answer. One of them was Wash. Elkins, and the other was Mr. John Crudip, who used to be the justice of the peace in Jefferson.

Question. Did you know any of the rest?

Answer. I knew Sid Lipscomb. He was in the band. I certainly knowed them three.

Question. Did they live in Jefferson?

Answer. Mr. Crudip lives there. Wash. Elkins lives two miles from there; and Sid Lipscomb about three miles.

Question. How many of those, whom you saw, had disguises on?

Answer. One of them had his face smutted, and another one had a knit cap on his face. He was a boy about four feet and a half high.

Question. What were they mad at your husband about?

Answer. He just would hold up his head and say he was a strong radical; he would hang on to that, and Wash. Elkins came here one time this summer, and went on his bond and carried him out to work on his plantation, and while my husband was in jail I went to Mrs. Norwood. He gave me a room for my washing and ironing, and when my husband got out of jail he wanted my husband to make me break my contract, and Saturday evening he got mad at my husband because he didn't make me break my contract, and then he put a chain on his neck and took him to George Whitfield's house, and they staid there all night; and Sunday they fetched him back to Jefferson again, and sent for me to come out there. I told them I wasn't going because I couldn't break my contract. He jumps over the fence and drawed that same pistol on me, and said he would blow my brains out. Ten or twelve white men were there; Reub. Bryant was there, and catched hold of his hand and told him he had better not hurt me. Mr. Norwood was standing there at the same time, leaning up against the fence, and I said I could prove by Mrs. Norwood that I made a contract to do the washing, and he said, "Don't tell me about Mr. Norwood; he is as damned a rascal as you," and he left me and catched hold of Mr. Norwood and drawed his pistol on him, and Mr. Norwood's wife went there and got him away from there.

Question. Who did this?

Answer. That was Wash. Elkins that was doing all this. He was Wash. Elkins's brother-in-law. He did this on Saturday evening because I wouldn't go. He came to the gate and told me, "Robin shall never do you no good; I'll never rest until I kill him." He told me that to my teeth, and I knowed they were going to kill my husband that week they killed him. I told him so, and I tried to get him out of Jefferson, but he said he hadn't done nothing and wouldn't go. They had promised to kill him, and I knew they were going to kill him.

Question. Was there a coroner's inquest held over your husband after he was killed?

Answer. Yes, sir. Lawyer Jackson, from Linden, was up there, and some other men; twelve were there in Jefferson beat.

Question. Were you examined as a witness?

Answer. Yes, sir.

Question. And your son?

Answer. Yes, sir; my son, too.

Question. What was done with any of those men who killed your husband?

Answer. They didn't do anything with them. They never made no botheration; they didn't seek after them. If they had sought after them they would have found some of them lying up with the lick my husband had struck with his dog-iron.

Question. You say no warrant was ever issued for the arrest of any of those men?

Answer. No, sir; they took our names down that we knew he was killed by a gun. That was all I could understand that was done. They didn't bother about anything else that I could see.

12

JAMES H. ALSTON

Montgomery, Alabama

October 17, 1871

James H. Alston, a prominent Republican politician in Macon County, Alabama, was believed to be so influential that Democrats offered him $3,000 to sway black voters to the Democratic party. The committee interviewed him about the violence in Macon County and his ultimate move to Montgomery to flee the threats on his life.

JAMES H. ALSTON (colored) sworn and examined.

By the CHAIRMAN:

Question. Where do you live?

Answer. I have been living here about sixteen months, but my place of residence is Tuskegee. I have been forced to live here for sixteen months.

Question. Your former place of residence was Tuskegee?

Answer. Yes, sir.

Question. How came you to leave there?

Answer. I was representative of that county, and I was caused to run away from there. I had to leave there to keep from being shot, and to keep my wife from being shot. . . . I have been shot. I have now in me buck and ball that injures me a good deal, and I think it will be for life; and my wife has been injured a good deal.

Question. Tell us first about your own case. State when you were shot.

Answer. I was shot, I reckon, about sixteen months ago. It was somewhere about May or June, 1870; I think it was June.

Question. Were you at home at the time?

Answer. Yes, sir; sitting on the side of my bed.

Question. Was in [*sic*] the day-time or night?

Answer. At night, about ten minutes before 1 o'clock at night, on Saturday night.

Question. Who did it?

Answer. Well, sir, it was done by a band of men, who were against my politics, as a republican.

Question. Were they disguised men?

Answer. Well, sir, so far as the disguisement was concerned, my shutters were closed, and I was in the house, and they fired through the windows; and I didn't see the men at the time.

Question. Had you a light in the house?

Answer. Yes, sir.

Question. Had you blinds to your windows?

Answer. Yes, sir.

Question. They shot through the blinds?

Answer. Yes, sir.

Question. And hit you in the back?

Answer. In the back and through the right hip.

Question. How many shots were fired?

Answer. Two hundred and sixty-five shots were counted outside in the weatherboarding of my house the next day, and sixty, as near as we could count, passed through the window, and five through the headboard of the bed I was sitting on, and two through the pillow that my head would have laid on, and four in the foot-roll of my bed, and two in my body.

Question. Was your wife hit?

Answer. Yes, sir, and one of my children. She was hit in her right heel, and it is lying in her foot now.

Question. Was she in the bed at the time?

Answer. Yes, sir.

Question. You did not see any of the men, you say?

Answer. Not at the time. I saw them before. They threatened my life before that.

Question. Did they come to your house on horseback or on foot?

Answer. They came on foot, sir.

Question. Did they demand admittance into the house?

Answer. No, sir, they shot from the gate right through the window.

Question. Was there a bright light in the house at the time?

Answer. Yes, sir.

Question. Was it the light made by the fire?

Answer. No, sir; I had a lamp with kerosene, pretty bright. It was struck just as I got in.

Question. You say you had been threatened before that?

Answer. Many a time.

Question. Who threatened you?

Answer. I was threatened by a good many white persons, and that night I was threatened by colored persons that they had appointed. They came into my lodge: I was made president of the lodge, or my club. I run against several white men—I reckon six of them—and by trying to be as I intended to be, a republican, I was looked upon well by the constituents I had there, and they elected me. I had in the lodge a white secretary. I was offered, by Mr. Robert Johnson, $3,000 to use my influence in the county against my constituency.

Question. What, in the legislature?

Answer. No, sir, in the county.

Question. To use your influence where?

Answer. To use my influence in my own county. I will tell you how it happened. I was appointed by Governor Smith, myself and the fellow called William Turner, at Wetumpka, to canvass the third district. He thought I could do some service with the party, I suppose.

Question. Governor Smith did?

Answer. No, sir, Mr. Johnson; he offered me $3,000 to use my influence in favor of the democrats.

Question. What did you tell him?

Answer. I told him that Jesus Christ was betrayed for thirty pieces of silver, only one to the thousand to what he offered me; that he wanted me to do the like; but that I wouldn't do it for $3,000 or to save my life; that I held my life more dear to me than anbody [*sic*] else, but I wouldn't betray my people to save my life.

Question. Who was Robert Johnson?

Answer. A gentleman that stays up in Tuskegee, in my place. Misfortunately he happens to be my wife's father, I believe. I don't know that, but I think he is.

By Mr. BLAIR:

Question. You think that Mr. Johnson is your wife's father?

Answer. Yes, sir. He wanted me to have something though; he was a democrat, and he thought $3,000 would help us a little if I would change my politics.

By the CHAIRMAN:

Question. What was your occupation?

Answer. I was a shoemaker before I was a musician. At that time I was a representative from that county.

Question. In the legislature?

Answer. Yes, sir. When I was shot I was a representative of the State.

Question. Did you have a good deal of influence with the colored people?

Answer. I had them every one, just from my authority; that is true. I used the influence; I was threatened every day, but I rode around and I got them all, and insured them as constituents with my authority; from my assurance to them that I had acted for them where they placed me as my constituents, I had them right with me to do whatever I wanted done in the county. I had that commission from the grand lodge, and I took a vote to that thing. I worked altogether by that, and I never varied from it a letter up to the time I was shot. . . .

Question. You were about telling the committee the cause of your being shot. You may go on now and state what warnings you received and the threats that were made.

Answer. I received a Ku-Klux letter from them once. I brought that down and gave it to the general in command here.

Question. What did they write to you?

Answer. That I had better leave—wait and let me get it together; it's a long time ago—that the bloody moon and the highway murderers was seeking my blood; that the tombs in the grave-yard was rumbling together against each other to receive my body—have you got the midnight robbers and murders down?—and I had better leave. Now, sir, I was told by a gentleman named Harper, in Tuskegee, that there was a letter of that kind in the office for me, which he knew all about. Mr. Harper—I hope you will take that name down, particularly— I told him I was a representative of the State then, and had a box, and I went for my letters every day; I didn't think I ought to be taught what time to go to the office. I went there and got the letter, and Mr. Phelps was the postmaster at that time in Tuskegee. I wanted him to notice that I got that letter out of the office.

Question. Did you show him the letter?

Answer. Yes, sir.

Question. Did you open it in the office?

Answer. No, sir. I opened it and handed it to the sheriff, and he read it, and after I took the letter out and handed it to the sheriff, and got him to read it—a gentleman by the name of Mr. Moore was the sheriff at that time; I don't know the initials of his name, but I think it was James Moore—after the letter was taken out, Mr. Henry Foster and Mr. Bill Dougherty, which is a republican now—he has changed since—met me on the street, and told me that they were Ku-Klux. In the day-time that was done; they had no disguises on; they had pistols though, plenty of them. One had four and the other had two. They told me that they had Jesus Christ tied, and God Almighty, the damned old son of a bitch, chained, and they were Ku-Klux. This was in the day-time. They told me that they were going to kill me, but if I would join the Ku-Klux they would spare my life. Then they asked me if I didn't see them leading Jesus Christ and God Almighty through Tuskegee as an elephant? I told them no, and if they were at the place I was at, in their beds, at that time of night, they would not have seen them. They persuaded me then to burn up the Ku-Klux letter that I had. I told them no, I would hand it over to the general, which I did. I told them I would bring it down to the general and wouldn't burn it, and I did so.

Question. What general was that?

Answer. I can't recollect now who was in command here at the time. It was the general that came after this cripple-man they had down here. I could tell in the morning which; I will make a report if you want it.

Question. Was that the only warning you had that the Ku-Klux were coming?

Answer. No, sir. My house is between the court-house and a church they call Zion church, which they posted it up on the bridge. I was compelled to cross over going to my house.

Question. What did they post up?

Answer. That if ever I attempted to cross the bridge, my throat should be cut, and that a damned nigger that was a republican should not live anywhere about them. I was persuaded by several of the citizens not to cross the bridge. I told them that on the thirteenth, fourteenth, and fifteenth amendments, I thought I had a right to cross any place that would lead me to property I had bought and paid for, and I would go. I crossed the bridge several nights, and the notice was there, but I never was attacked.

Question. Did you receive any other notice?

Answer. Gentlemen, there's only three things I want to say: I want you to understand what General Battle, the gentleman I was with in the command, which bought me as a slave and carried me into the army, and even went near enough to send on the capital at Washington, General Battle—I suppose you have heard of the name—I want to tell you what he said to me the second or third night after I was shot.

Question. Were you a soldier in the war?

Answer. Well, sir, I was for awhile with them, because I was a slave.

Question. In the confederate army?

Answer. Yes, sir.

Question. Did you carry a musket?

Answer. No, sir: I always have been a musician. . . . They forced me to enlist then. I will tell you what General Battle did. The sheriff of Macon, Mr. Paget, after I was shot, Sunday morning, got that—that, I think, is the most particularest thing you gentlemen has got; that is, his action with me, a colored man. The probate judge of the county, on the Sunday morning after I was shot, came to my house. His name is Mr. Mennifee. He told me that I attempted to celebrate the fifteenth amendment; which I did. I will own that. He wanted to show me that a nigger couldn't hold no office in that county no longer, and he knew that I was going to be shot; that a nigger wasn't fit for nothing else than to drive oxen, and drive the carriage of white folks. I refused then to have any arrests made of men that had threatened my life the night before. I told them I couldn't get justice, and I didn't want any arrests to be made. He brought the soldiers there, and forced me to make arrests of the men that shot me, or threatened my life, formed a counsel for me against my wishes, which was a white man that had lost all his property on account of the fire, and I had some property, and he wanted to get hold of my house and lot. They had me taken out. After two days after I was wounded they took me out of my house and hauled me in the wagon, in the rain, to the court-house, and they examined me from 8 o'clock in the morning until 6 in the evening, drawing gallowses and everything before me to keep from getting in the right evidence that I knowed, but it didn't effect [*sic*] nothing with me. They told me I had made myself so conspicuous in the county, I made my way to Washington, which I did. I went to Washington, sir, and I came back, and they said, "We intend to kill you before you shall rule this county any longer." . . .

Question. Was that in Macon County?

Answer. Yes, sir.

Question. I thought that was in Tuskegee?

Answer. It was in Macon County; Tuskegee is the county-seat of Macon County.

Question. You had to run?

Answer. Yes, sir; I run and staid in the swamp ten days.

Landownership, Economic Success, and Displacement

13

ELIZA LYON

Demopolis, Alabama

October 24, 1871

Eliza Lyon, an ex-slave from Demopolis, Alabama, testified before the congressional committee in her hometown about the murder of her husband, Abe Lyon. During the attack, out of fear, she took her two children to the woods, leaving all their possessions and money behind. She never returned home.

ELIZA LYON (colored) sworn and examined.

By the CHAIRMAN:

Question. What is your name?

Answer. Eliza Lyon; my husband went by that name after the surrender. He used to belong to Mr. Lyon before the surrender. He went by the name, after that, of Abe Smith, but they still call him Abe Lyon.

Question. Where do you live?

Answer. Here in Demopolis; I was raised here.

Question. Have you ever been married?

Answer. Yes, sir.

Question. Where is your husband now?

Answer. He was killed.

Question. When was he killed?

Answer. The 6th of June.

Question. Of this present year?

Answer. Yes, sir.

Question. In what county was he killed?

Answer. Choctaw County.

Question. Were you with him at the time?

Answer. Right with him in the bed.

Question. Were you living in Choctaw at the time?

Answer. Yes, sir.

Question. On whose plantation?

Answer. Dr. McCall's.

Question. You may describe how your husband was killed.

Answer. They knocked on the door; it was about 11 o'clock at night. We never had heard of any threats of his life, and were not thinking of such a thing. They came on Tuesday night, the 6th of June. They knocked on the door; they knocked on the gallery [porch], and asked was Abe Lyon in, with a loud voice, and he answered, yes, he was, and he got up, not thinking anything about anybody going to disturb him, and looked out of the door. I said, "Don't go out, Abe; it sounds like more voices than one." He jumped up and looked out of the door; the bed was right at the door. As he looked out they told him to come out, but I jumped up and shut the door, and pushed him away from the door; I shut it, and told him to go out of the other door. He went to the door to go out; but some of the children had buttoned the door lower down, and he could not find the button,[1] for it was dark, and he was so scared; and he wheeled around in the room in his scare, and I was scared too; and then I went to unbutton the door. He passed me going to the same door, intending to get out, but he looked like he was in a perfect scare, standing in the floor, and I run behind him for him to go out, and as I run up, the men burst the door open and threw a rope right over his head and drew his arms down to him, and picked him up deliberately and toted him out. I holloed and screamed for help, but no one came near. We were not living near people, but lived close enough for them to hear loud holloing. After they picked him up and carried him out, I still stood on the gallery holloing, and four men—white men—came up to me, and one held his gun here on each side of my head, and one in my face, and one right here in my chest, and they told me if I didn't hush holloing they would blow a hole through me. I took my hand and knocked the gun off a little bit; they didn't shoot me then; they told me never mind, hold on, they would finish me directly. They had carried Abe off then, around and up a little hill to kill him. They killed him about as far off as across the street here to the hotel.

Question. In what way did they kill him?

---

[1] An oblong or elongated piece of wood or metal, which turns on a pin or screw.

Answer. They shot him with a double-barreled gun. I run from this end of the gallery to that end, to see when they shot him. The first shot was a double-barreled gun. At the next one, someone holloed to them all to fire, and all fired, I reckon. I will not reckon about it, for the holes was counted they shot in him; and Dr. McCall counted thirty-three holes they shot in him. After I saw they had shot him, I saw them coming back to the house. I knew they were going to kill me, as they had told me they would. I thought I would go in the room and wake my children up, and take them up; and when I came out of the room there was about seventy-five men at the door, guarding me regularly—all white men. I could see into their faces; they were standing so close to me. As I was standing there, they walked off around the house, and called the other men to come on, and let's finish in the house; and while they stepped around the corner of the house, I went in the room and picked up one of the children; the other was wakened, but the other was out and gone. I picked up the one that was asleep, and run out of the gate at the corner of the house, and went off across the new ground or field, and run for about a quarter of a mile, and stopped in a thicket of woods to see what they were going to do. I made my child sit down, and I stood up to see them. They came back to the house, and went around and in the house, and tore up everything. Then they made a light, and went under the house with a light, and in the house, and in the hen-house, and in the stables. They must have been looking for me; I don't know what else. Then I took my children and went farther in the woods. They shot off all the pistols in the house, and shot my dog, and then came out and shot off their pistols and guns, and it sounded like there was over a hundred shots at once. . . .

Question. Was any of your property in the house stolen that night?

Answer. We had some money on Monday looking at it. I had a daughter up here, and was sending her to school; besides, I had three children at home. We had some money in the house, but I don't know whereabouts he put it, but we had it in a little square box about a foot long and half as wide, and I reckon that had about $600 in it; we were looking over it, and I wanted some of it to bring up here to school my daughter on it. Then I says, "Put it away till we get over chopping the cotton, and then I will go; you can spare it." I was going to bring it up here; I had no idea of anybody killing him. He took it and put it away, and I went to sleep. I do not know whether he put it in the blacksmith-shop, or under the house, or where. If it was in the house, or under it, they got it. I do not know where he put it, for I was satisfied he could get it. I never have seen it. I left my hogs and wagon and everything.

Question. How long after your husband was killed before you came away?

Answer. He was killed Tuesday night, and I left Sunday morning for the river to take the boat.

Question. Had you staid at your house all the time?

Answer. No, sir, I moved right out, for I thought they would come for me; I went to a neighbor's house.

Question. Did you miss anything else besides the money?

Answer. No, sir, nothing besides the money. I left my hogs down there, and left a wagon we had paid $75 for, and we had a great many other little things.

Question. Why did you not bring your things away with you?

Answer. They had threatened my life, and he had been killed, and I could not tell how or what nor nothing about his business.

Question. Who has your property?

Answer. I just left it there; I suppose I never will get it; I am afraid to go back.

14

WARREN JONES

Atlanta, Georgia

October 27, 1871

Warren Jones, an ex-slave who was brought to Warren County, Georgia, from North Carolina before the Civil War, spoke to the congressional committee in Atlanta. Jones testified that he was run out of the county by the Klan, who threatened his life after he demanded his share of the crop he and a white business partner had raised.

WARREN JONES (colored) sworn and examined.

By the CHAIRMAN:

Question. State your age, where you were born, and where you now live.

Answer. I was thirty-nine years old the 15th of last February. I was born in North Carolina, and was brought away in my youth, by a speculator, to Warren County, Georgia, and I now live in Atlanta.

Question. When did you leave Warren County?

Answer. The 20th of last March.

Question. Why did you leave there?

Answer. They got so bad I could not stand it; they threatened to take my life. The gentleman who I was working with—

Question. Who was he?

Answer. Obadiah Laseter.

Question. What was he going to take your life for?

Answer. He said I should not leave him; he wanted me to work with him for nothing. I had worked with him and made thirty bags of cotton, and he promised to give me half. I went to him, after I made the crop, and asked for some pay to support my family. He said I should stay there and work for nothing. I said I could not stand it. He said if I undertook to leave he would Ku-Klux me.

Question. Who are the Ku-Klux?

Answer. Men who go about and take advantage of black people, I suppose. He went to a gentleman in the neighborhood, and told him he was going to take my life. That gentleman came to me and said that I had better make my escape, because Mr. Laseter had said he would kill me certain. At that time the Ku-Klux were very thick. They came to my house once; they came into the yard and stopped. I had an understanding the day before, and they did not find me. I gathered up what I could in my arms, and, with my wife and child, I came away.

Question. How long did you work there?

Answer. From the 4th of one March until the 20th of the next March.

Question. How much did he give you?

Answer. Nothing. I had right smart of money when I commenced, and I hired all the labor, and paid for all the labor. He was to give me half, and furnish all the stock and the land; but he did not give me anything. . . .

Question. What reason did he give for not letting you have what belonged to you?

Answer. He thought if he did I would be able to live without his assistance; and it is the law down there that a colored man shall have nothing without going to a white man.

Question. Do you mean the law of the State of Georgia?

Answer. No, sir; it is their law. They have no law there, except what they make themselves, for colored men to go by. When I came here I did not have a cent in the world. . . .

Question. Did this Mr. Laseter hire any hands?

Answer. No, sir.

Question. You did all the work yourself?

Answer. Yes, sir.

Question. Did you furnish half the feed for the horses?

Answer. Yes, sir; and I did all the shop-work; he was to pay me for half of that.

Question. He is owing you for half the crop and half the shop-work?

Answer. Yes, sir.

By Mr. BAYARD:

Question. Has the crop of cotton been baled?

Answer. Yes, sir, and sold.

By the CHAIRMAN:

Question. Had it been sold before you left there?

Answer. Yes, sir; he had the last bill for it when I went to him for my pay.

Question. Do you know how much the thirty bags of cotton sold for?

Answer. The first seven bags, weighing 502 pounds each, on the average, sold for 14¾ cents per pound. The last picking weighed 501 pounds, on the average, and they sold for 14½ cents a pound.

Question. What are you doing here?

Answer. I am working at the coal-yard.

15

SAMUEL TUTSON

Jacksonville, Florida

November 10, 1871

In the post-emancipation New South, vigilantes targeted economically successful, landowning blacks nearly as much as they pursued black and white Republican politicians. Samuel and Hannah Tutson (Document 7) were attacked in Clay County, Florida, for not vacating their property. In the attack, Klansmen beat the couple severely and also tore down their home.

KKK Testimony, 13:54–59.

SAMUEL TUTSON (colored) sworn and examined.

By the CHAIRMAN:

Question. What is your age, where were you born, and where do you now live?

Answer. As near as I can come at it, I am between fifty-three and fifty-four years old; I was born in Virginia, and I now live in Clay County, seven miles from Waldo, on the Santa Fé [River].

Question. How long have you lived there?

Answer. I left there this year; since May.

Question. Where did you live before that?

Answer. On Number Eleven Pond, in Clay County.

Question. Are there any people in your county that they call Ku-Klux?

Answer. They called themselves Ku-Klux that whipped me that night.

Question. What night was that?

Answer. I do not know hardly what night it was; but they whipped me like the mischief.

Question. What month was it?

Answer. It was in May.

Question. How many were there?

Answer. There were nine; five swung on to me, and four to my wife.

Question. At what time in the day or night was it?

Answer. It was between midnight and day.

Question. Were they disguised; and if so, how were they disguised?

Answer. They blacked their hands and blacked their faces.

Question. Was there any change made in their clothing?

Answer. No, sir; one came in in his shirt-sleeves, but all the rest had on their coats.

Question. Tell us what they did when they came, and all that was done.

Answer. They came to my house, and my dog barked a time or two, and I went out and could see nobody; my wife went out and could see nobody at all; we had not more than got into the house and got into bed, when they came and flung themselves against the door, and it broke loose on both sides, and fell right into the middle of the floor; my wife said, "Who's that?" Then George McCrea made to her, and I made to her to help her; as I did so, some one standing by the door caught me by my right arm, and I could not get to her; they pulled and pulled, and tried to pull me away, but they could not, and then they dragged my feet from under me and flung me down across a cellar-door and near broke my back; they dragged me over the fence, and broke down five or six panels, and took me away down the hill on the side of a hammock, and tied me to a pine and whipped me.

Question. How many lashes did they give you?

Answer. It is out of my power to tell you.

Question. How many of them struck you?

Answer. Well, they blindfolded me for a time; Dave Donley struck me over the eye before I got to the place where they tied me, and they stamped on me and kicked me; he was the first one who whipped me after I was tied, and Bob Lane was the next one who struck me.

Question. How many licks did they strike you?

Answer. I cannot tell you; they hit me a whole parcel of times.

Question. Who struck you?

Answer. Cabell Winn struck me with a pistol and choked me, and ran my head up against the tree, and told me that if it was not for sin, he would blow my "God-damned brains out." He said that I pulled down my fence, and let people's stock in my fields, and killed them. I said, "You can't prove it." He said he could prove it on my "God-damned back."

Question. Who else struck you?

Answer. All struck me; but the rest I did not see, for I was blindfolded when the rest struck me. When they ran my head up against the tree, I could see Bob Lane, and Dave Donley, and Cabell Winn.

Question. Did they blindfold you before they began to whip you?

Answer. Yes, sir; and they stripped me just as naked as your hand; they took every rag off of me, and took my shirt and tore it up, and took a piece and blindfolded me, and then took another piece and twisted it up, and put it into my mouth, like a bridle-bit, so that I could not holler.

Question. Were you standing up?

Answer. All the time.

Question. Did they tie you to anything?

Answer. They made me hug a tree and tied my hands together.

Question. When they got through whipping you, what did they do?

Answer. They went and tore down my house, and said that they were going to whip us as long as they wanted to; and then they were going to tie us up by the thumbs and let us hang awhile; and then hang us by the neck until we were dead; and then fling us into Number Eleven Pond.

Question. Did they untie you when they were done whipping you?

Answer. They did not untie me when they got done their whipping, but I got loose while they were tearing down my house. Two of them staid there, and the rest went to the house, and when my wife broke loose, they ran to her, and I got clear.

Question. Who whipped your wife?

Answer. All of them; she can tell you about that more than I can.

Question. How far from the house did they take you to whip you?

Answer. As near as I can come at it, it was about a quarter of a mile.

Question. What did they whip you for—what did they have against you?

Answer. Because I would not give up my land to Mr. Winn. I bought a man's improvements [to the land], a man by the name of Free Thompson. Mr. Tire and Mr. Thompson were first cousins. After Thompson was gone with my money that I let him have for his improvements, Tire came there and said that it was his land. I asked him why he did not let me know when I first came there, and he said he wanted me to do a heap of work there before he bothered me. I said, "Are you going to give me anything at all for what I gave for the land?" He said, "No." I said, "Are you going to give me anything for the crop in the ground?" He said, "No." I said, "Are you going to give me anything at all for the improvements I have put on?" He said, "No." Then I said, "Is there any law here for kinky heads?" He said, "Yes, there is." I said, "No, there isn't." He said, "Yes; there is as much law for you as for me." I said, "Then, if there is any law for kinky heads, I will find it." He tried a right smart while to get me away, and I would not go; and Mr. Winn took it to get me away from there.

16

AUGUSTUS BLAIR

Huntsville, Alabama

October 9, 1871

Augustus Blair, a landowner in Huntsville, Alabama, told the congressional committee about the brutal attack on his son one evening in December 1868. After the attack, he and his family were forced to leave their property.

KKK Testimony, 9:674–79.

AUGUSTUS BLAIR (colored) sworn and examined.

By the CHAIRMAN:

Question. Where do you live?

Answer. Here in Huntsville.

Question. Where did you live in December, 1868?

Answer. On Major Floyd's plantation, in Limestone County, on Fort Hamilton Hill. . . .

By the CHAIRMAN:

Question. State whether you had a son killed about that time—December, 1868.

Answer. Yes, sir.

Question. Go on and state the circumstances of his death.

Answer. I had a son who was living with me at the time; the only son I had; about eighteen years old; very well grown; as big as I was. He went out on a Monday night over to what they called the Allen's Ford, where some colored people were settled, on the creek, hog-killing, and Jim Henry Cox, and Bunk Hinds and Pony Hinds, (two brothers,) were there, and they got into a row with this boy.

Question. Who did?

Answer. These Hinds and Jim Henry Cox, and then Jim Henry Cox tried to cut his throat with a knife, and he throwed up his hand, and some other colored people—Place Forrow and Reuben Blair—prevented it, and they took him home with them that night, and he came to his house Tuesday morning to me, and the Tuesday night following the Ku-Klux came. They told him that night, "You fight now, but you will not fight when the Ku-Klux come." It was awful cold that night.

Question. Did the Ku-Klux come to your house?

Answer. Yes, sir. . . .

Question. How many came in?

Answer. Sim Hudson and Pony Hinds walked in at the door, and just behind them came Hugh Hudson, Sim Hudson's father, and he took a chair and sat down by the fire, and they ordered me to light a candle. I took a candle from the mantelpiece and pulled a straw from the broom to light the candle. Sim Hudson kicked his father a little in the back with his knee, and pointed to me. I was looking in his face this way. I knew him. I had lived there thirty years.

Question. Had they disguises on?

Answer. Only one of the men had; Dick Hinds had on a disguise. I knew him. Me and him was raised together. He had a little piece over his face. They came and searched my house all over it. By the time I got out of bed I heard them breaking the door down in the room where my boy was, with two grown daughters. He had two sisters that were grown; they had been married, but their husbands died in the war. They broke that door down, and just as I got up I heard the door fall, and they said, "Here he is, by God! Here he is!" Dick Hinds came into my house and asked me to carry the candle into the next room, and one of them said, "Keep back Jim Henry; he will cut his throat." I walked in and says to my daughter, "Where's William?" and she says, "There he is; see the blood running"; and I stepped out on the platform and held up the candle and looked at them, and as I looked out two of them had him and had his head drawn back in this way (illustrating) and two others were beating him in the face with a pistol. They had no disguises on. They finally took him off a quarter of a mile. . . . As they went through the yard I went through the orchard and got over where there was hogweeds as high as my head, and came up and heard their conversation as they were going up the hill with my boy. On the hill there was some cotton, and I got on my knees there and crawled up to hear what they would do; for if they killed him I wanted to find him. There they stripped him naked. I was close enough to hear him, as they were going up, when he told them, "Oh! gentlemen, you all carrying me along, and here are two men stabbing me with a knife." They said, "It's a damned lie; nobody is sticking you." He says, "Oh, yes; I feel the blood running down my pants." They says, "Go on, God damn you; you will have no use for no blood no how mighty soon." He went on up the hill with them, and they were punching and cutting him. When they got up there they took him down and beat on his head. I was not further from them than twenty yards. I crept right around behind the patch of briars and laid there. He never hollered but once, but I could hear him [imitating the wheezing, rattling sound in the throat] as they were choking him, and others were cutting him with a knife as they held him there, and some of the rest of them were going backwards and forwards to the other company, and some of them came sometimes as close as from here to that post, [five yards.] I would lie close, so they could not see me. The night was mighty cold, and they made up a fire just a piece off—as far off as from here across the street—and they would pass backward and forward; and one of them says by and by, when they were cutting at him, "The captain says you have done enough." They said to the boy, "You feel here and see how you like these gashes. Do you reckon they will do you?" He went back to the captain and told him, and the captain hollered, "I told you to spare life," [*sic*] and then one says, "Get up, get up, God damn you," and I looked up, and the boy was so weak that when he went to get up he was staggering, and one of them catched him by the shoulders and held him, and just then one hauled off and struck at him. He had staggered, I reckon through weakness, for the road was bloody all the way up the hill. This man hauled off and struck him and then jumped on to him and stamped him, and they shot off their pistols then and got on their horses and went away. I was looking at them to see which way they were going for a while, but I got uneasy and went on to take the boy on to the house. I was scrambling in the bushes and around trying to find him, when I heard the girls, a quarter of a mile off from me, cry out, "Oh, Lord! Lord! here's Billy cut to pieces with a knife! Come, sister, help me put him in the house." And I struck and ran home, and there he was standing with nothing on him but his shirt, and trembling all over and bloody, and I says, "Oh, what's the matter? Can't you tell me nothing, my boy?" and he says, "No, no," and they took him in and I drew the bed before the fire in my room and sent the little boy off as fast as he could go for the doctor, but the doctor sent word he was going to Huntsville and could not come. The next morning before day I put the little boy on a horse and sent for the doctor again. Doctor Frank Blair sent word he couldn't come, but he would send his father, old Doctor John Blair; that was the man that raised me. He never came until 8 or 9 o'clock that morning; then he walked in. By that time the house was crowded with white people, and when he walked in and looked at the boy he says, "I don't think I can do him any good." Says I, "Are you going off without trying to do him any good, doctor?" He says, "Have you got any tallow?" I told him I had. He says, "Have you any castile soap?" I said, "Yes," we had. Says he, "Have you got any tar?" I told him we had. Then he turned in and made a poultice, a salve, and dressed his wounds. I heard him tell it in Huntsville afterward that it took him two hours to dress the boy's wounds. You couldn't touch him anywhere, from his shoulders down to the tips of his big toes. There was no place on his legs or feet that you could touch him.

Question. Why could you not touch him?

Answer. Because it was cut to pieces with a knife. The calves of his legs were split up and cut across, and his thighs were split open and cut across, and his knee looked like they had tried to take the cap off of his knee, and all his hands and arms were cut and slit up too. . . .

. . . These men, when they came back to my house asked, "Where is Gus?" She [his wife] said she didn't know, and they knocked her down, and stamped her and choked her on the bed. They went down to the house to one of my daughters and choked her and beat her, and was going to beat Eliza, but she begged that she was sick and says, "I don't know where father is." One of them run in the house then and said, "Come out here and let the women alone; they don't know where Gus has gone."

Question. How long was that after your son was taken out?

Answer. The same night. A parcel of them took him and two of them came back and did that, and they told my wife, "Tell Gus he has been here two years, and it is as long as we intend he shall be here. White folks wants to work this land." There is six hundred acres of land cleared. I rented out part of my land there to a white man named Mr. Wallace. He told my wife to tell me that inside of two weeks I must not be caught there. He said, "He has got to get away, crop or no crop."

Question. Were these men all renters?

Answer. The Hudsons were renters. They were not all renters. Dick Hinds had a very good plantation. The Hudsons were renters, and Jim Henry Cox and Ruff Ray were renters. Then I had to just get away from there as quick as I could.

Black Autonomous Institutions: Schools and Churches

17

HENRY GILES

Montgomery, Alabama
October 17, 1871

As part of the Ku Klux Klan's agenda to maintain white supremacy, Klansmen destroyed black churches, places of autonomy for most black communities, in all the southern states. Henry Giles, a deacon of an African American Baptist church in Nixburg, Alabama, testified before the committee regarding the threats that he and his congregation received from the Klan. Politics also played an important role in the harassment,

---

as it often did: Giles noted that Klansmen targeted the church for the congregation's Republican leanings. Giles ultimately had to flee the county, and his family was stripped of all its property.

HENRY GILES (colored) sworn and examined.

By the CHAIRMAN:

Question. Are you ever called Garrett?

Answer. No, sir; not now. . . . I went by that name when I first registered. . . .

Question. Where do you live now?

Answer. Here in Montgomery, since Christmas. I could not go back home to see my folks.

Question. Where did you live before Christmas last?

Answer. In Nixburg beat.

Question. In what county is that?

Answer. Coosa.

Question. How long did you live in that county?

Answer. Near about twenty years.

Question. Were you a deacon of a colored Baptist church in Nixburg beat?

Answer. Yes, sir.

Question. Tell the committee what you know about the burning of that church — when and how it happened, and who did it.

Answer. I will, as near as I can. They said we were too strong republicans.

Question. Who said that?

Answer. Jesse Thomas and all them white men in the beat; that was the word that they sent to me. Jerry Webb said, about two months before they burned the church, "I know the men that is going to burn down this church, but no man can make me tell."

Question. Who did he tell that to?

Answer. To the whole crowd, on Sunday, two months before it was burned.

Question. That he knew who was going to burn it down?

Answer. Yes, sir; and that nobody could make him tell.

Question. How long had the church been built?

Answer. Better than a year, I think.

Question. Who built it?

Answer. We all built it.

Question. Was it a colored church?

Answer. Yes, sir; and the colored people built it.

Question. Go on and state the particulars of its being burned down.

Answer. Sam Maxwell, when we first began to meet there Sundays, said we should not have meeting there. It was dangerous, because of the threats; they would take us some nights when we couldn't tell; that the Ku-Klux would come there, and kill us all some of these nights, and we would have no warning of it. Then from that there was a general report all the time—we might expect that these Ku-Klux would come, but we didn't know when they would come. "But you, Henry Giles, we intend to give you more particular than the rest." That was the understanding that come to me, because I was head deacon of the church, that they intended to get me, and to burn me up in the church.

Question. Go on and state what took place about the burning of the church.

Answer. They said, "We ain't got nothing against you, only you all are too strong republicans"—that is the great misfortune we have at that beat—"and we intend to break up this arrangement of the republicans in Coosa County."

Question. Who said that?

Answer. That was general report with all the colored population whenever they get them. We run a mighty risk when we were going to Nixburg to the polls to vote.

Question. What day was that?

Answer. The day of the election.

Question. Last fall?

Answer. Yes, sir.

Question. What kind of risk did you run?

Answer. Why we expected some of us to get killed on the way.

Question. Did anybody threaten you?

Answer. Yes, sir; all the time before the election and after the election.

Question. What kind of threats?

Answer. Because we voted the republican ticket.

Question. Were these threats against all the colored people there?

Answer. Yes, sir.

Question. Did they all vote the republican ticket that went to the polls?

Answer. Yes, sir; all voted it when I was there, but I didn't stay long, and the crowd that went with me came away; they were uneasy anyhow.

Question. Did the white men say anything to you?

Answer. No, sir; the white party was for a fuss with the colored party, and we didn't stay more than half an hour after we voted. We left as quick as possible.

Question. Was that last fall?

Answer. Yes, sir.

Question. When was this church burned?

Answer. The 1st of January; it was the last Saturday night in the Christmas: that was the . . . 1st of January, I think. Christmas came on Sunday, and the next Saturday night it was burned down, and Sunday night I came down here, and I haven't been back there since.

Question. Did you see the church burning?

Answer. Yes, sir.

Question. How far did you live from the church?

Answer. I reckon about five hundred yards. I saw them when they set fire to it.

Question. How many men did you see at the church?

Answer. It appeared to me like it was about sixteen. I was close to them, but I had to hide down pretty close; but I saw them.

Question. Are you afraid to return?

Answer. Yes; unless there is a better arrangement.

Question. Did you leave any property?

Answer. Yes, sir; and my family; my wife and seven children in the family.

Question. And you are afraid to go back and live with your family for fear that these Ku-Klux will molest you?

Answer. Yes, sir. Here is a letter I have received from my wife. [Exhibiting a letter.]

Question. You say they have made threats that they would kill you if you went back?

Answer. Yes, sir; that's the fair understanding.

Question. You have been working here?

Answer. Yes, sir; they stripped me of everything since I came here.

Question. Who stripped you of your property?

Answer. I couldn't tell. My wife said they just took everything.

Question. What property did they take?

Answer. They took a cow and calf from me, and my corn and my meat I had there—a piece—and all.

Question. How was it taken; was it generally stolen after night from the place, or in what way was it taken?

Answer. She said it was taken in the day-time. She sent me word so.

Question. Did she know who took it?

Answer. Yes, sir.

Question. Were they neighbors?

Answer. No, sir; the neighbors are not close by.

Question. On what ground did they take them?

Answer. I don't know. They had no fear, because they had run me off, and they took it as they pleased. I don't know the men that took them from me. They did it because I was too strong a republican, and they would do anything to injure me.

Question. Did any white men ever tell you that?

Answer. No, sir.

Question. You gathered that from others?

Answer. Yes, sir; I got the report. They wouldn't tell me themselves, but I got the report of what they intended to do with me, gentlemen.

Question. Who would bring you that word; white men or colored men?

Answer. Charley Carter fetched that word to me the last morning— Sunday morning—that Jesse Thomas said he couldn't get me on Saturday night, but intended to get me the coming week. He was the head of the Ku-Klux band.

18

CORNELIUS McBRIDE

Washington, D.C.

July 21, 1871

Cornelius McBride, a white schoolteacher born in Belfast, Ireland, who had traveled to Mississippi to teach in a black school, testified before the committee in Washington, D.C., about the makeup of the Ku Klux Klan in his area and the details of a host of local attacks. McBride was harassed and terrorized by the Klan in Chickasaw County, Mississippi, for educating black children. Ultimately, he had to flee the region.

CORNELIUS McBRIDE sworn and examined.

By the CHAIRMAN, (Mr. POLAND:)

Question. Where do you live?

Answer. I live in Chickasaw County, Mississippi.

Question. How long have you lived there?

Answer. Nearly one year.

Question. From where did you go when you went there?

Answer. From Oktibbeha County, an adjoining county.

Question. How long had you been in that county?

Answer. Nearly one year.

Question. Where did you reside before that?

Answer. In Cincinnati, Ohio.

Question. Are you a native of Ohio?

Answer. No, sir.

Question. Where were you born?

Answer. I was born in Belfast, in the north of Ireland.

Question. For what purpose did you go to Mississippi?

Answer. To teach school.

Question. Did you teach school in Oktibbeha County?

Answer. Yes, sir.

Question. You taught there for about a year?

Answer. Yes, sir.

Question. What sort of a school?

Answer. A colored school. . . .

Question. What is the character of the men who belong to this Ku-Klux organization, so far as you know them or have heard of them?

Answer. As a general thing they are an ignorant, illiterate set of men, and they seem to be determined to keep everybody else the same. The men who are engaged in Ku-Kluxing, if they were not sympathized with by men of better standing than themselves, would soon go under.

Question. Can you give an idea of the amount of sympathy, or the character of aid and assistance, they got from men of property and standing?

Answer. Yes, sir; it is easily shown. In the matter of bail, or anything of that kind, the best men in the community will give their signatures. In Oxford, for instance, when those men were arrested and brought there they were put in pretty good quarters among the soldiers. But the people of the county had a meeting for their benefit, and took them beds and chairs, and playing cards, and all that. That showed the sympathy of the people with them. And when the United States marshal was struck there, they showed their sympathy by arming themselves and going into the court-room.

Question. Can you, from reliable information, give any idea of the number of the Ku-Klux in your county, and in other counties there?

Answer. We believe that about one-half of the white people in our county belong to the organization.

Question. What induces you to believe that?

Answer. From the fact that if you denounce the Ku-Klux, or take any action against them, you make one-half of the people there your enemies, and they show it by condemning you. The president of the board of supervisors in my county asked me what kind of evidence I had against these fellows; I told him that I had several colored witnesses and some white witnesses. He said, "You must not bring colored testimony against white men in this county."

Question. Have you any other facts going to show the number of men who belong to this organization?

Answer. Those men who whipped me told me there were five millions of them in the United States; I believe that was the number.

By Mr. BECK:

Question. How many?

Answer. Five millions they said. . . .

By Mr. COBURN:

Question. . . . Have you given a statement of all the acts of outrage perpetrated by these men, that have come to your knowledge? If not, give such as you have omitted to state, that have occurred in your county and in adjoining counties.

Answer. I know of the whipping of Colonel Huggins. I know from reports of other men being whipped; in some cases I saw the men themselves; in some cases I got the information from other persons. I saw the wife of Aleck Page; her husband was taken out and killed in Monroe County. Dupree was murdered in that county, and a number of others. In fact the cases are so many that I cannot remember them all. I have a number of cases noted here, which I can give; I got the statements from the parties themselves.

Question. That is what I want to get at. If you have any reliable information in relation to such matters, state what it is.

Answer. This information comes from the parties themselves, or from Mr. Wiley Wells, the United States district attorney at Oxford.

Question. Do you mean by "themselves," the victims of the outrages?

Answer. Yes, sir. Addy Foster was whipped in Winston county for buying land.

By Mr. BECK:

Question. State in each case how you got the information.

Answer. I got this from William Coleman, his neighbor; William Miller told me that he was whipped because they said he would not raise his hat to a white man; he was there before the grand jury at Oxford.

Question. In what county was that?

Answer. That was also in Winston County. Aleck Hughes, in Noxubee County, was whipped. A white man owed him $17, and he threatened to sue him for it, and they whipped him for doing so. Aleck Hughes gave me the statement himself.

By Mr. COBURN:

Question. Are you giving instances where the outrages were perpetrated by disguised white men? That is what I am inquiring about.

Answer. Yes, sir; all those cases were by disguised men. They hung Aleck Hughes up by the neck and nearly killed him; he was insensible when they let him down. Zack Job was whipped in Noxubee County, and Henry Leadbetter was also whipped; both by disguised men.

By Mr. BECK:

Question. State when it was done.

Answer. I do not know when; it was done some time in March. In Corinth, Mississippi, George Shubble was also whipped by disguised men; and near the same place Fanny Honeysuckle was whipped by disguised men; and Mr. Campbell, who kept a grocery store, was whipped by this body of disguised men, because he would not give them some whisky.

By Mr. COBURN:

Question. In Corinth?

Answer. In Corinth, or near Corinth. A number of other men at Oxford told me of outrages committed upon them; but I omitted to note the counties.

Question. No matter about them. You have testified as to the hostility of the people to free schools. What is the cause set forth by those men for their hostility to free schools?

Answer. Well, educating the colored people is the great cause of objection; that is the reason why they are against free schools; and then it is a republican measure. If the democratic party had passed that bill, I am sure there would not have been any opposition to it in that State, except on the part of a few white people who might have objected to being taxed to support colored schools. The great opposition to it is because "it is a damned radical free-school system"; that is the way it is spoken of.

Question. Is it from an apprehension that the negro will become equal to white men; or is it from hostility to the negro, and a desire to keep him down; or is it both?

Answer. It is both.

Question. Have you heard any expression of opinion in relation to that? [I]f so, state it.

Answer. I will give the expression of a lady in our neighborhood. She said that a white man who taught a colored school ought to be hung; that he should not show his face among white people.

Question. Why?

Answer. Because it was disgraceful to teach a colored school; and a white man dare not visit the house of a colored man there on any account, or they would not allow him to visit a white family again.

19

ELIAS HILL

Yorkville, South Carolina

July 25, 1871

Elias Hill, a Baptist minister and teacher in York County, South Carolina, was dragged outdoors and beaten with a buggy whip by a group of Klansmen. Hill was attacked for his role as a minister, as well as his participation in the Republican party and the local Union League. Union Leagues, also called Loyal Leagues, began in the North during the Civil War to mobilize support for the war effort and the Lincoln administration. After the war, and especially after the start of Radical Reconstruction, these organizations spread throughout the South. They raised funds for mutual aid societies, organized cooperatives, and advised freedpeople on contracts with landowners. Hill's assailants were particularly concerned with what he was telling local blacks behind closed doors in meetings and during church services, such as encouraging them to leave York County to find opportunities denied them in the region.

KKK Testimony, 5:1406–16.

ELIAS HILL (colored) sworn and examined.

By the CHAIRMAN:

Question. Where do you live?

Answer. In Clay Hill precinct in this county, (York.)

Question. How long have you lived there?

Answer. I was born and raised there. I was born belonging to the Hills, near the mill—just above the mill.

Question. How old are you?

Answer. Fifty years. I was born in May, 1819.

Question. How long have you been in your present crippled condition?

Answer. I was afflicted and became disabled from walking when I was seven years of age. I walked until I was seven.

Question. Since that time have you been as badly afflicted as you are now?

Answer. I continued to get gradually worse from that time until the present.

Question. How long is it since you were able to walk?

Answer. It is forty-five years since I walked.

Question. How long is it since you have been in your present condition?

Answer. One arm was drawn up directly after I was taken down.

Question. What disease was the cause of that?

Answer. The doctor said it was rheumatism.

Question. How were you maintained?

Answer. My father bought himself some thirty-odd years ago, by paying $150 to the estate of the Hills, and that made him free; and when my people were sold, he bought my mother, but he could not get her without taking me; as I was a cripple, they compelled him in the contract to take me when he bought his wife, who was my mother.

Question. Then you were not a slave?

Answer. I was born a slave, but never served.

Question. Can you read and write?

Answer. Yes, sir.

Question. When and how did you learn that?

Answer. I learned that gradually, between the years 1830 and 1845, from the school children, and catching it up as I could. Between those years I became so much of a scholar as I am.

Question. State whether at any time men in disguise have come to the place where you live, and, if so, what they did and said. First, state when it was.

Answer. On the night of the 5th of last May, after I had heard a great deal of what they had done in that neighborhood, they came. It was between 12 and 1 o'clock at night, when I was awakened and heard the dogs barking, and something walking, very much like horses. As I had often laid awake listening for such persons, for they had been all through the neighborhood, and disturbed all men and many women, I supposed that it was them. They came in a very rapid manner, and I could hardly tell whether it was the sound of horses or men. At last they came to my brothers [*sic*] door, which is in the same yard, and broke open the door and attacked his wife, and I heard her screaming and mourning. I could not understand what they said, for they were talking in an outlandish and unnatural tone, which I had heard they generally used at a negro's house. I heard them knocking around in her house. I was lying in my little cabin in the yard. At last I heard them have her in the yard. She was crying, and the Ku-Klux were whipping her to make her tell where I lived. I heard her say, "Yon is his house." She has told me since that they first asked who had taken me out of her house. They said, "Where's Elias?" She said, "He doesn't stay here; yon is his house." They were then in the yard, and I had heard them strike her five or six licks when I heard her say this. Some one then hit my door. It flew open. One ran in the house, and stopping about the middle of the house, which is a small cabin, he turned around as it seemed to me as I lay there, awake, and said "Who's here?" Then I knew they would take me, and I answered, "I am here." He shouted for joy, as it seemed, "Here he is! Here he is! We have found him!" And he threw the bedclothes off of me and caught me by one arm, while another man took me by the other and they carried me into the yard between the houses, my brother's and mine, and put me on the ground beside a boy. The first thing they asked me was, "Who did that burning? Who burned our houses?" [G]in-houses, dwelling-houses and such. Some had been burned in the neighborhood. I told them it was not me; I could not burn houses; it was unreasonable to ask me. Then they hit me with their fists, and said I did it, I ordered it. They went on asking me didn't I tell the black men to ravish all the white women. No, I answered them. They struck me again with their fists on my breast, and then they went on, "When did you hold a night-meeting of the Union League, and who were the officers? Who was the president?" I told them I had been the president, but that there had been no Union League meeting held at that place where they were formerly held since away in the fall. This was the 5th of May. They said that Jim Raney, that was hung, had been at my house since the time I had said the League was last here, and that he had made a speech. I told them he had not, because I did not know the man. I said, "Upon honor." They said I had no honor and hit me again. They went on asking me hadn't I been writing to Mr. A. S. Wallace, in Congress, to get letters from him. I told them I had. They asked what I had been writing about? I told them, "Only tidings." They said, with an oath, "I know the tidings were d——d good, and you were writing some-thing about the Ku-Klux, and haven't you been preaching and pray-ing about the Ku-Klux?" One asked, "Haven't you been preaching political sermons?" Generally, one asked me all the questions, but the rest were squatting over me—some six men I counted as I lay there. Said one, "Didn't you preach against the Ku-Klux," and wasn't that what Mr. Wallace was writing to me about. "Not at all," I said. . . . After they had staid in the house for a considerable time, they came back to where I lay and asked if I wasn't afraid at all. They pointed pistols at me all around my head once or twice, as if they were going to shoot me, telling me they were going to kill me, wasn't I ready to die? and willing to die? didn't I preach? that they came to kill me—all the time pointing pistols at me. This second time they came out of the house, after plundering the house, searching for letters, they came at me with these pistols, and asked if I was ready to die. I told them that I was not exactly ready; that I would rather live; that I hoped they would not kill me that time. They said they would; I had better prepare. One caught me by the leg and hurt me, for my leg for forty years has been drawn each year, more and more year by year, and I made moan when it hurt so. One said, "G——d d——n it, hush!" He had a horsewhip, and he told me to pull up my shirt and he hit me. He told me at every lick, "Hold up your shirt." I made a moan every time he cut with the horsewhip. I reckon he struck me eight cuts right on the hip bone; it was almost the only place he could hit my body, my legs are so short—all my limbs drawn up and withered away with pain. I saw one of them standing over me or by me motion to them to quit. They all had disguises on. I then thought they would not kill me. One of them then took a strap and buckled it around my neck and said, "Let's take him to the river and drown him." "What course is the river?" they asked me. I told them, east. Then one of them went feel-ing about, as if he was looking for something, and said, "I don't see no east! Where is the d——d thing?" as if he did not understand what I meant. After pulling the strap around my neck, he took it off and gave me a lick on my hip where he had struck me with the horsewhip. One of them said, "Now you see I've burned up the d——d letter of Wal-lace's and all," and he brought out a little book and says, "What's this for?" I told him I did not know; to let me see with a light and I could read it. They brought a lamp and I read it. It was a book in which I had kept an account of the school. I had been licensed to keep a school. I read them some of the names. He said that would do, and asked if I had been paid for those scholars I had put down? I said no. He said I would now have to die. I was somewhat afraid, but one said not to kill me. They said, "Look here! Will you put a card in the paper next week like June Moore and Sol Hill?" They had been prevailed on to put a card in the paper to renounce all republicanism and never vote. I said, "If I had the money to pay the expense, I could." They said I could borrow, and gave me another lick. They asked me, "Will you quit preaching?" I told them I did not know. I said that to save my life. They said I must stop that republican paper that was coming to Clay Hill. It has been only a few weeks since it stopped. The republican weekly paper was then coming to me from Charleston. It came to my name. They said I must stop it, quit preaching, and put a card in the newspaper renouncing republicanism, and they would not kill me; but if I did not they would come back the next week and kill me. With that one of them went into the house where my brother and my sister-in-law lived, and brought her to pick me up. As she stooped down to pick me up one of them struck her, and as she was carrying me into the house another struck her with a strap. She carried me into the house and laid me on the bed. Then they gathered around and told me to pray for them. I tried to pray. They said, "Don't you pray against Ku-Klux, but pray that God may forgive Ku-Klux. Don't pray against us. Pray that God may bless and save us." I was so chilled with cold lying out of doors so long and in such pain I could not speak to pray, but I tried to, and they said that would do very well, and all went out of the house except one. . . .

Question. How many of these men were there?

Answer. Six.

Question. How were they disguised?

Answer. With coverings over their faces. Some had a kind of check disguise on their heads. One had black oil-cloth over his head, and something like gloves covering his hands and wrists. When they brought the lamp to read that little book I could see his face all around his eyes, and he seemed a red-whiskered man.

Question. Did you know any of them?

Answer. No, sir, I cannot say I know any one of them.

Question. Who was this red-whiskered man?

Answer. From what I have heard since I believe it was a Max Steele, who lives right below us.

Question. Are you confident of it, or is it a mere opinion?

Answer. From what I have heard since, to the best of my knowledge it was him.

Question. From what you saw there?

Answer. No, sir, I only saw through the eye-holes of his disguise.

Question. Had you been president of the Union League?

Answer. Yes, sir. They charged that, and I owned it.

Question. Had there been political meetings held at your house?

Answer. Yes, sir, and I owned that; but they were not this year.

Question. Had you been preaching?

Answer. Yes, sir, regularly.

Question. For how long?

Answer. Every month. I have been preaching regularly for some ten years or more, with a license to preach.

Question. To what church do you belong?

Answer. To the Baptist church.

Self-Defense

20

WILLIS JOHNSON

Columbia, South Carolina

July 3, 1871

Willis Johnson, a laborer in Newberry County, South Carolina, explained to the committee how he defended himself when a group of Klansmen came to his home.

WILLIS JOHNSON (colored) sworn and examined.

By the CHAIRMAN:

Question. Where do you live?

Answer. At Leonidas Sims's, in Newberry County.

Question. How long have you lived there?

Answer. This year. I lived there one year since I have been free before this year.

Question. What is he?

Answer. A planter.

Question. Are you a laborer?

Answer. Yes, sir.

Question. Can you read and write?

Answer. No, sir.

Question. Were you taught any before you were free?

Answer. No, sir.

Question. Have you been taught any since?

Answer. No, sir.

Question. Have you been at any time visited by men masked and disguised — Ku-Klux?

Answer. Yes, sir.

Question. When?

Answer. Last night two weeks ago.

Question. Go on and tell what you saw and what they said and did, telling it in your own way.

Answer. When I awoke, as near as I can tell, it was between 12 and 1 o'clock. I heard some one call "Sims." I held still and listened, and heard them walk from his door to my door. I was up-stairs, and I got up and came down-stairs. They walked back to his house again and asked him to put his head out. He did not answer, but his wife asked them who they were. They said they were friends. They walked back to my door again, and just as they got to the door they blew a whistle. Another whistle off a piece answered, and then men seemed to surround the house and all parts of the yard. Then they hallooed, "Open the door." I said nothing. I went to the head of the bed and got my pistol, and leaned forward on the table with the pistol just at the door. They tried with several surges to get the door open, but it did not come open. They went to the wood-pile and got the ax, and struck the front door some licks, bursted it open, and then went to the back door and burst it open. Nobody had yet come into the house; they had not come in. They said, "Strike a light." Then I dropped down on my knees back of the table, and they struck some matches and threw them in the house, and two of them stepped in the front door, and that brought them within arm's length of me as they stood there. As soon as they did that, I raised my pistol quickly, right up to one's back, and shot, and he fell and hallooed, and the other tried to pull him out. As he pulled him I shot again. As they were pulling, others ran up and pulled him out in the yard, and when the whole party was out in the yard I stepped to the door and shot again, and then jumped to the back door and ran. I got off. I staid away until the next morning; then I came back and tracked them half a mile where they had toted this man and laid him down. I was afraid to go further. Mr. Sims and I were together, and I would not go any further, and he told me to go away; that I ought not to stay there; that he saw the men and saw the wounded man, and was satisfied that he was dead or mortally wounded, and I must leave. Mr. John Calmes, the candidate of the democrats for the legislature, advised me to take a paper and go around the settlement to the white people, stating that I would never vote the radical ticket, and he said he did not think they would interfere with me then. He said that all they had against me was that on election day I took the tickets around among the black people; and he said, "You knocked me out of a good many votes, but you are a good fellow and a good laborer, and we want labor in this country." I told him I would not do that.

Question. Had you taken any part in politics?

Answer. I only had tickets on the day of the election, and I had given them out.

Question. Had you been active in getting colored voters to go to the election?

Answer. Yes, sir; I had done right smart that day.

Question. Did these men tell you what they wanted you to come out for?

Answer. They never said a word why. They did not ask me to come out, but to open the door.

Question. Were they disguised?

Answer. I did not see the disguises. I dropped down under the table when they opened the door; but Mr. Sims said he saw them disguised.

Question. Did you see this man who fell?

Answer. He fell just as the matches went out; I had no time when I shot to see his face, and as they were going out I shot again.

Question. Do you know of anything that was charged against you except the part you had taken in politics?

Answer. Nothing at all.

Question. Had you had a quarrel with anybody?

Answer. Nobody.

Question. Who is Mr. Sims; is he a republican?

Answer. He was a democrat; I was working for him.

Question. You say you heard them call for him, and ask him to come out?

Answer. Yes, sir; he did not make them any answer; his wife answered them.

Question. Did you say you were in the same house?

Answer. No, sir; I was in a separate building.

Question. In the quarters?

Answer. My house was his cook-kitchen, about twenty yards from his house.

Question. Are you married?

Answer. Yes, sir; I had my wife and three children in the house. They are there now.

Question. Did you leave then in pursuance of that advice?

Answer. Yes, sir.

Question. Are you afraid to go back?

Answer. Yes, sir; of course I am. Mr. Sims told me, and several other white people, on Monday, that they were satisfied that if I did not leave there they would kill me some time or other, and his advice was for me to leave then. He did not want me hurt, I suppose.

Question. How many persons were there?

Answer. From what I saw I suppose there were fifteen or twenty. He says he saw the whole party before when they began to break in and after they left, and there were fifteen or twenty.

Question. Did you track them by the blood?

Answer. No, sir; by the tracks through the oats patch.

Question. Was there any blood in the path by which they went away?

Answer. No, sir.

Question. Do you know whether this man was killed or not?

Answer. I do not; Mr. Sims said when they put him over the palings [fence], one of them said, "God damn it, hold up his head." Six of them went off toting him.

Question. Had you any previous notice that these people were coming?

Answer. Yes, sir; they had put up a paper that I was to leave in fifteen days. That was three months ago.

Question. Where was that put up?

Answer. On Duncan's Creek bridge.

Question. What kind of a notice?

Answer. It was a notice. They put Mr. Sims's name on the paper, and my name, "Willis Johnson," and said, "He had better get away from here; we give him fifteen days to get away."

Question. Was it signed?

Answer. No, sir; only his name and mine, saying I had fifteen days to get away.

By Mr. Van Trump:

Question. In what connection did they use Mr. Sims's name with yours?
Answer. That was where I was living.

By Mr. Stevenson:

Question. How do you know that it was the Ku-Klux that did it?
Answer. That was what the white folks said; I could not read it.

By the Chairman:

Question. How far is Simms's [*sic*] place from Newberry?
Answer. Fifteen miles. It is near the line of Union County.
Question. Have there been any other people whipped or shot in that neighborhood?
Answer. Not in the neighborhood. There had been notices put up for others to leave. That was the same time mine was put up. Mr. Calmes advised them to take a paper and go around the settlement and the white people would sign it, and then they could stay there, and they did it.
Question. What kind of a paper was it?
Answer. It was a paper promising not to have anything to do with the republican party any more, and advising everybody to have nothing to do with it.

By Mr. Van Trump:

Question. You did not take such a paper as that around?
Answer. No, sir.
Question. It was Mr. Sims's opinion, then, after you had shot this man, that that would make everything right?
Answer. Yes, sir; Mr. Calmes did. . . .
Question. Do you think you killed that man?
Answer. I do not know.
Question. Was there any blood?
Answer. No, sir; but he fell at the crack of the pistol, and they pulled him out and laid him down outside of the door, and when I ran out he was still lying there.
Question. You do not know whether he was playing possum or was hurt?
Answer. I think he was hurt, because I put my pistol right on him at the center of his back and fired, and he fell.

21

BENJAMIN F. HERR

Livingston, Alabama

October 31 and November 1, 1871

During his testimony about the violence in his county and the rise of the Union League in the region, Benjamin Herr, called by the minority, told the committee about an incident in which a large group of African Americans defended themselves against a group of night riders.

BENJAMIN F. HERR sworn and examined.

The CHAIRMAN. This witness being called at the instance of the minority, I will ask General Blair to examine him.

By Mr. BLAIR:

Question. Captain Herr, please state your residence and occupation.
Answer. Livingston, Sumter County, Alabama. I hardly know what my occupation at present is. I have been an editor and publisher until within a month or two.
Question. How long have you resided here?
Answer. Since 1865. I located here after the surrender, in the spring of 1865.
Question. Where were you born?
Answer. Lancaster, Pennsylvania. I was raised there.
Question. Did you come immediately from Pennsylvania here?
Answer. No, sir; I removed to Missouri in 1853, and resided there until 1861. . . .
. . . During the day, or night, some one (as has been alleged) whipped a negro. The circumstances attending this whipping we have not been able to learn.

But, at all events, the party assaulted, instead of appealing to the law, busied himself in arousing the anger of his colored friends; and the night following, a number of them, armed, collected at his house. This fact excited apprehensions of a disturbance, and a small party of whites took it upon themselves to watch the premises. During the night one of them, named Melton, approached the house, and, just as he entered the yard, was shot down. After falling, another volley was fired at him. Hoping to escape further injury thereby, he feigned death, and, both parties believing he was dead, the one ceased firing, and the other withdrew and gave the alarm. On the day following (Sunday) a number of whites assembled at Belmont, some of them much excited. It was finally determined, however, to proceed under due process of law, and a warrant was issued for the arrest of the parties who had shot Melton. It was given to an officer at a late hour in the day, and he, being fearful that the blacks might attack him before he could make known to them his business and authority, declined executing until next day. A man named Collins, a bridge-builder employed at this place, offered to execute the process forthwith. It was given to him, and, accompanied by a small party of young men, he set out. Arriving opposite the house in which the negroes were, the party dismounted in the road, and Collins and two or three others proceeded towards the house. Just as they entered the yard, Collins being second, they were fired on from ambush. Collins fell dead, and two of his companions were slightly wounded. The arresting party returned the fire, but the negroes, having reloaded, discharged another volley, and the whites retired, leaving the body of Collins where he fell.

This occurrence added fuel to the excitement previously existing, and the news spreading, large numbers of whites, from various parts of the country, flocked to Belmont. The negroes also received re-enforcements, and took position in an almost impenetrable swamp, in the vicinity.

A portion of the whites urged an immediate attack on the negroes; but cooler heads assumed control, under authority of the sheriff. Two unarmed men were detailed to demand the body of Collins of the negroes, but it was with difficulty the latter could be induced to allow them to approach; and when they did so, and made the demand, the blacks replied that their leader had gone to Demopolis, and if they wanted Collins's body before he returned, they (the whites) must fight for it. This was on Monday.

It now seemed that a conflict was inevitable; and the whites, their number constantly augmenting, began preparations for a determined attack. The next day, however, and that want of justification might not be urged, another demand was made for the body of the murdered man. This time it was surrendered, with the assurance from the blacks that they only gave it up "because it smelled so bad." They refused to surrender any of his personal effects.

The whites now organized and prepared for a dislodgment of the blacks on the next day, at all hazards, subject to the authority of the sheriff.

It was about noon on Wednesday before those in command directed a forward movement, the force having been deployed so as to include within its field of action all the territory held by the blacks. But, as they advanced, no negroes were found—they pushed on to the river, but no force was encountered. The blacks had (in view of the preparations made, and of which they doubtless had information) concluded that discretion was the better part of valor; and on the night previous, as was subsequently ascertained, had disbanded and fled.

There being no further necessity for their presence, the whites quietly dispersed and returned to their homes—some of them no little chagrined because, as they believed, time had been consumed unnecessarily, and the blacks had escaped merited punishment for their deeds of violence, and defiance of lawful authority.

22

EDMUND W. PETTUS

Washington, D.C.

July 6, 1871

Edmund W. Pettus, a former U.S. court of appeals judge from Alabama, came to Washington, D.C., at the request of the minority, to provide the congressional committee with details of vigilante violence in his state. During his testimony, he outlined an incident in which African Americans rallied to their own defense and took the law into their own hands.

KKK Testimony, 8:374–403.

Edmund W. Pettus sworn and examined.

The Chairman, (Mr. Poland) As this witness has been summoned by the minority of the committee, he will be first examined by some member of the minority.

By Mr. Blair:

Question. Where do you live?

Answer. I reside in Selma, in the State of Alabama.

Question. How long have you resided in the State of Alabama?

Answer. I was born in Alabama, and have lived there ever since. I am now fifty years old.

Question. What public positions have you held in the State?

Answer. I was solicitor of the seventh circuit for ten or twelve years, and I was a judge of the same circuit for four years. Those are the only civil positions I ever held.

Question. That was before the war?

Answer. Yes, sir.

Question. State the general condition of affairs at this time in regard to the security of life and property in the State, especially in the region with which you are most familiar, and the manner in which the law is enforced.

Answer. At this time I believe the law is reasonably well enforced in the State of Alabama, and that life and property are as safe there as they have ever been at any time within my knowledge.

Question. Do you know of any secret organization in the State, political or otherwise, whose purpose or practice is to violate the law, and uphold each other in the violation of the law?

Answer. I have never known of any such organization myself. Do you desire I should speak of what I know, or of what I have heard?

Question. Give us any information that you have upon which you place reliance. You can speak not only from your own knowledge, but from information upon which you rely.

Answer. There have been disorders of a very serious character in Alabama. After the war the floating bad population of both armies to some extent was there, and there were great disorders; and I have no doubt, from information, that there were parties combined together to commit disorders. But, so far as I know or am informed, I think they were local organizations, for local purposes, and very bad purposes. There is also, as I am informed, (and I have no doubt of it from information,) a political organization of the colored people which is also to some extent engaged in the same sort of purposes. I think, however, in its original formation it was designed for merely political objects and has been perverted by bad men to the same bad purposes.

Question. Have any of these disturbances occurred in your immediate neighborhood or in the section of country in which you practice?

Answer. No, sir. I live near the center of the State; and so far as I know there have been no violations of law by combinations except in two instances, and I think that they were the result of immediate excitement; that they did not probably originate from any preconcerted plan except an arrangement to act on the spur of the occasion—a combination to meet the emergency when it arose. There were two such occurrences in my immediate vicinity.

Question. What were those?

Answer. The negroes had been very much exasperated by the killing of a negro policeman in Selma by a man named Wright, and also by the killing of a man named Frank Diggs on the Meridian train—a private assassination. This man Diggs was a black man who had something to do with the mail; I do not now remember his connection with it. He was a popular man with the white people, and also with the negroes; he was a well-behaved man and a man of good character. These occurrences had produced very great excitement among the negroes in the neighborhood where I live, and they manifested a hostility toward any one who should in any way commit any wrong toward any one of their race. In other words, they were combined for the purpose of retaliation. In that state of feeling a young man named Baxley and a colored man named Alfred Granger, two journeymen brick-masons, quarreled and fought on the streets in Selma—those two alone. The colored man was killed. Baxley was arrested by the officers of the law and taken in the direction of the calaboose [local jail]. Just before they got to the calaboose the negroes in large numbers (I suppose there were some four or five hundred when they first seized him) took him away from the officers, beat him over the head, dragged him up and down the public streets by the heels and cut his throat, and stabbed him in several places. The officers of the law did their best, so far as I saw, to prevent it, without force; but in a mob of that kind the ordinary police force is of no effect. We finally gathered an armed force, and went there. I had charge of it myself. When they saw us coming, they drew off a short distance, ready for a fight as it appeared; but we were merely intending to protect this man's life if we could. There was a great deal of cursing and insult, just such as a mob would heap on a party of men coming, as they considered, in hostility to them. But there was no bloodshed. We got between them and the house where they had finally carried this young man.

Question. You rescued the young man from them?

Answer. I cannot say that, because before we got to the spot the violence had ceased, and the young man had been left for dead. He was not dead, however, and ultimately, after being confined in jail for several months, he recovered.

Question. Was anything done to punish the rioters?

Answer. Yes, sir; some of them were arrested, and I think two of them have been convicted—two or three, I do not recollect which.

Ku Klux Klan: Members, Apologists, Makeup, and Character

23

NATHAN BEDFORD FORREST

Washington, D.C.

June 27, 1871

Nathan Bedford Forrest, a former general in the Confederate army, is often considered the founder of the Ku Klux Klan. He went before the congressional committee to discuss the organization, its activities, and his involvement. Despite admitting that he received fifty to a hundred letters a day about the Klan or similar groups, he denied any involvement in the Klan and at times denied the organization's very existence. Forrest and many of his colleagues in the Klan told the truth only as much as they thought necessary when they testified; otherwise, they resorted to evasion, claims of having a poor memory, and outright lying.

KKK Testimony, 13:3–41.

N. B. FORREST sworn and examined.

By the CHAIRMAN:

Question. Where is your residence?

Answer. My residence is in Memphis, Tennessee. . . .

Question. In what business have you been engaged?

Answer. I am president of two railroads that we are trying to build in that country; they are now consolidated, but have been two up to within the last few days.

Question. Has your business brought you in contact, to a large extent, with the people of the country through which your road passes?

Answer. Yes, sir, it has.

Question. We desire to ascertain the manner in which the laws are executed in the Southern States, and the security there enjoyed for person and property. So far as your observation enables you to speak, will you state what are the facts in that respect?

Answer. So far as I know, I have seen nothing that prevented the law from being executed; I have not seen anything at all to prevent the laws from being executed.

Question. Do you know anything of any combinations of men for the purpose either of violating the law, or preventing the execution of the law?

Answer. I do not.

Question. I have observed in one of the Western papers an account of an interview purporting to have been had with you in 1868, in which you are reported to have spoken of the organization of what was called the Ku-Klux in Tennessee, their operations, their constitution, the numbers of the organization; and also a correction in one or two particulars afterward made by you of the facts stated in that interview. You recollect the article to which I refer?

Answer. Yes, sir.

Question. Upon what information did you make the statement in regard to the organization and constitution of the Ku-Klux in Tennessee?

Answer. Well, sir, I had but very little conversation with that party.

By Mr. VAN TRUMP:

Question. Do you mean with the reporter?

Answer. With the reporter. He misrepresented me almost entirely. When he came to see me he was introduced to me by another gentleman. I was in my office, suffering with a sick headache, to which I am subject at times, so that I was disqualified from doing anything. I was just going to my residence, and I said to him that I had nothing to say. That was the most of the conversation that occurred betwixt us. I remember talking to him may be three or four minutes. He asked me if there was an organization in Tennessee, and I told him that it was reported that there was. That, I think, was about the conversation that we had in regard to the organization. So far as the numbers were concerned I made no statement.

By the CHAIRMAN:

Question. I will call your attention specifically to the report of the interview, as reported in the Cincinnati Commercial of Tuesday, September 1, 1868; also to a letter in the paper, dated Memphis, September 3, and published in the paper of September 6, the letter purporting to have been written by yourself. In the interview, as reported in the paper of the 1st of September, these sentences occur:

"'In the event of Governor Brownlow's calling out the militia, do you think there will be any resistance offered to their acts?' I asked.

"'That will depend upon circumstances. If the militia are simply called out, and do not interfere with or molest any one, I do not think there will be any fight. If, on the contrary, they do what I believe they will do, commit outrages, or even one outrage, upon the people, they and Mr. Brownlow's government will be swept out of existence; not a radical will be left alive. If the militia are called out, we cannot but look upon it as a declaration of war, because Mr. Brownlow has already issued his proclamation directing them to shoot down the Ku-Klux wherever they find them, and he calls Southern men Ku-Klux.'

"'Why, General, we people up North have regarded the Ku-Klux Klan as an organization which existed only in the frightened imaginations of a few politicians.'

"'Well, sir, there is such an organization, not only in Tennessee, but all over the South, and its numbers have not been exaggerated.'

"'What are its numbers, General?'

"'In Tennessee there are over 40,000; in all the Southern States they number about 550,000 men.'"

Is there any other portion of that statement incorrect than the portion to which you called attention in your letter?

Answer. Well, sir, the whole statement is wrong; he did not give anything as it took place. So far as numbers were concerned, I knew nothing about the numbers of the organization. It was reported that there was such an organization in Tennessee, in fact throughout the United States; but I knew nothing about its operations.

Question. I will read your correction on that point in the letter of the 3d of September. In that letter you say:

"I said it was reported, and I believed the report, that there are 40,000 Ku-Klux in Tennessee; and I believe the organization stronger in other States. I meant to imply, when I said that the Ku-Klux recognized the Federal Government, that they would obey all State laws. They recognize all laws, and will obey them, so I have been informed, in protecting peaceable citizens from oppression from any quarter."

Is that the correction which you make of the statement that I read to you in regard to your saying that there were 40,000 Ku-Klux in Tennessee?

Answer. I made that statement. I believed so then, for it was currently reported that there were that number of men.

Question. That correction goes to the number; that you believed it was so reported, and that you believed there were 40,000 Ku-Klux in Tennessee. Upon what authority did you make these statements that the organization existed?

Answer. I made it upon no authority, nothing of my personal knowledge at that time. . . .

Question. I find in the report of that interview another statement, as follows:

"'But is the organization connected throughout the States?'

"'Yes, it is. In each voting precinct there is a captain who, in addition to his other duties, is required to make out a list of names of men in his precinct, giving all the radicals and all the democrats who are positively known, and showing also the doubtful on both sides and of both colors. This list of names is forwarded to the grand commander of the State, who is thus enabled to know who are our friends and who are not.'"

I do not remember that there is in your letter any correction of that statement.

Answer. Well, sir, I made no such statement at all to this man as that.

Question. Did you correct that statement in your letter?

Answer. I do not know whether it was corrected in the letter or not. If it was not, I wish to do it here. I made no such statement. I did not have as much conversation with him as you and I now have had. There were gentlemen there who heard what was said. I was suffering very much with a headache at the time, and told him I could not talk to him, that I did not wish to talk to him. He asked me a few questions.

Question. Is this statement as reported in the account of that interview a correct statement:

"'Can you or are you at liberty to give me the name of the commanding officer of this State?'

"'No; it would be impolitic.'"

Answer. No, sir; I never made that statement. I have received a letter from that reporter, acknowledging that he did misrepresent me. I do not have it here. Afterward, when he wrote another letter stating that he went with me to Fort Pillow, and that I had shown him where the negroes were killed, and how the battle was fought, he went on to make statements of all the facts, which statements were entirely false. I had never traveled with the man ten feet in my life.

Question. Is the whole account of this interview a misrepresentation?

Answer. Not all of it. I told him that I believed there was an organization in Tennessee, and that it had been reported 40,000 strong. I told him that; I said that. . . .

Question. Is this statement in that account correct:

"'Do you think, General, that the Ku-Klux have been of any benefit to the State?'

"'No doubt of it. Since its organization, the leagues have quit killing and murdering our people. There were some foolish young men who put masks on their faces and rode over the country, frightening negroes; but orders have been issued to stop that, and it has ceased. You may say, further, that three members of the Ku-Klux have been court-martialed and shot for violations of the orders not to disturb or molest people.'"

Is that statement correct?

Answer. No, sir; not the last part of it.

Question. That is, as to the shooting of three members of the Ku-Klux?

Answer. No, sir; that is not correct.

Question. Is the other portion of it correct?

Answer. A portion of it is.

Question. That orders had been issued to stop using masks?

Answer. I did not say that orders had been issued, but that I understood orders had been issued. I could not speak of anything personally.

Question. Well, with your assent, I will put the whole of this account of the interview, and your letter of correction, into the testimony. . . . I will now ask if, at that time, you had any actual knowledge of the existence of any such order as the Ku-Klux?

Answer. I had, from information from others.

Question. Will you state who they were who gave you that information?

Answer. One or two of the parties are dead now.

Question. Who were they?

Answer. One of them was a gentleman by the name of Saunders.

Question. Did he reside in Tennessee?

Answer. No, sir; he resided in Mississippi then. He afterward died by poison at Asheville, North Carolina.

Question. Did any other person give you that information?

Answer. Yes, sir; I heard others say so, but I do not recollect the names of them now. I say to you, frankly, that I think the organization did exist in 1866 and 1867.

Question. In what portions of the country?

Answer. I do not think it existed anywhere except in Middle Tennessee. There may have been some in a small portion of West Tennessee; but if there was any, it was very scattering.

Question. Under what name is it your belief it existed at that time?

Answer. Some called them Pale Faces; some called them Ku-Klux. I believe they were under two names.

Question. Had they an officer known as a commander?

Answer. I presume they did.

Question. Was their organization military in its character?

Answer. No, sir; I think not.

Question. Were they subject to command and drill in any military form?

Answer. They were like the Loyal Leagues, and met occasionally and dispersed again. The Loyal Leagues existed about that time, and I think this was a sort of offset gotten up against the Loyal Leagues. It was in Tennessee at the time; I do not think it was general.

Question. Had it a political purpose then?

Answer. I think it had not then; it had no political purpose.

Question. You say it was organized like the Loyal Leagues, or in opposition to them?

Answer. I think it was in opposition.

Question. Was the purpose of the Loyal Leagues political?

Answer. I do not presume it was; I do not know what it was.

Question. What did you understand to be the purpose of the two organizations?

Answer. I can tell you what I think the purpose of the organization that you first spoke of was; I think it was for self-protection.

Question. You mean now what is called Ku-Klux?

Answer. Yes, sir; I think that organization arose about the time the militia were called out, and Governor Brownlow issued his proclamation stating that the troops would not be injured for what they should do to rebels; such a proclamation was issued. There was a great deal of insecurity felt by the southern people. There were a great many northern men coming down there, forming leagues all over the country. The negroes were holding night meetings; were going about; were becoming very insolent; and the southern people all over the State were very much alarmed. I think many of the organizations did not have any name; parties organized themselves so as to be ready in case they were attacked. Ladies were ravished by some of these negroes, who were tried and put in the penitentiary, but were turned out in a few days afterward. There was a great deal of insecurity in the country, and I think this organization was got up to protect the weak, with no political intention at all.

Question. Do I understand you to say that the Loyal League organization in Tennessee countenanced or promoted crimes of the kind which you have mentioned?

Answer. I do not know that they promoted them; but these crimes were not punished; there was very little law then.

Question. Was this before the organization of the State government, or did it continue afterward?

Answer. Well, it continued so for a year afterward.

Question. How long, according to your information, did this Ku-Klux organization exist?

Answer. I think it was disorganized in the early part of 1868.

Question. Did it continue until after the presidential election?

Answer. No, sir; I think it was in the latter part of 1867, or the early part of 1868; I do not know the exact date.

Question. Where can we get the information as to the manner of its dissolution and the time of it?

Answer. I do not know where you can get it. I never got any positive information except that it was generally understood that the organization was broken up.

Question. Who were understood to belong to it?

Answer. Men of the Southern States, citizens.

Question. Did they speak to you without hesitation of the organization, as if it required no concealment?

Answer. No, sir; they did not.

Question. Did they deny or admit its existence?

Answer. They did not do either; they did not deny it or admit it. It was understood though, among the southern people, that this organization had disbanded about the time of the nomination of candidates for President of the United States.

Question. When they proceeded to carry out the objects of the organization, did they do it in numbers, by riding in bands?

Answer. I do not know; I never saw the organization together in my life; never saw them out in any numbers, or anything of the kind. . . .

Question. Did they go in disguise?

Answer. I suppose some of them did.

Question. Was that the general understanding?

Answer. That was the rumor.

Question. Did they proceed to the extent of whipping or killing men?

Answer. I heard of men being killed, but I did not know who did it.

Question. Was it done by these persons in disguise?

Answer. Well, yes, sir; there were men killed in Tennessee and in Mississippi by bands in disguise. There were men found down there disguised, white men and negroes both. . . .

Question. Then I understand you to say that this whole statement, giving the idea that you knew of your own knowledge of the organization of the Ku-Klux, or that you knew of their numbers or their discipline, is incorrect?

Answer. I never said to that man that I knew anything about it.

Question. Had you ever a constitution of the order?

Answer. I saw one; yes, sir.

Question. Where was that?

Answer. That was in Memphis.

Question. Who had it?

Answer. Well, it was sent to me in a letter.

Question. Have you that constitution yet?

Answer. No, sir.

Question. What has become of it?

Answer. Well, I burned up the one I had.

Question. Who sent it to you?

Answer. That I cannot tell.

Question. Did it come anonymously?

Answer. Yes, sir; it came to me anonymously.

Question. What was the purport of it?

Answer. The purport of that constitution, as far as I recollect it now, was that the organization was formed for self-protection. The first obligation they took, if I recollect it aright, was to abide by and obey the laws of the country; to protect the weak; to protect the women and children; obligating themselves to stand by each other in case of insurrection or anything of that sort. I think that was about the substance of the obligation. . . .

Question. What was the name of the organization given in that constitution?

Answer. Ku-Klux.

Question. It was called Ku-Klux?

Answer. No, sir; it was not called Ku-Klux. I do not think there was any name given to it.

Question. No name given to it?

Answer. No, sir; I do not think there was. As well as I recollect, there were three stars in place of a name. I do not think there was any name given to it.

Question. That is, when it came to the name there was a blank, and stars in the blank?

Answer. Yes, sir.

Question. Signifying that the name was to be kept secret?

Answer. You are to place your own construction on that.

Question. That is the way it stood—the name of the organization left blank, and stars in its place—that is the way it stood in the constitution?

Answer. Yes, sir.

Question. Have you any idea how that came to be sent to you?

Answer. No, sir; I do not know how it came to be sent to me.

Question. From what point was it sent?

Answer. It was mailed from some place in Tennessee; I do not recollect now what point it was mailed from. I was getting at that time from fifty to one hundred letters a day, and had a private secretary writing all the time. I was receiving letters from all the Southern States, men complaining, being dissatisfied, persons whose friends had been killed, or their families insulted, and they were writing to me to know what they ought to do. . . .

Question. Did you act upon that prescript?

Answer. No, sir.

Question. Did you take any steps for organizing under it?

Answer. I do not think I am compelled to answer any question that would implicate me in anything. I believe the law does not require that I should do anything of the sort. . . .

Question. You say that whatever organization of Ku-Klux, or anything else, took place in the region of country with which you are familiar, it was gotten up through fear of depredations by the militia, and was the result of that state of things?

Answer. That is my understanding of it.

Question. And for the protection of themselves where the law was considered powerless?

Answer. According to my understanding, the organization was intended entirely as a protection to the people, to enforce the laws, and protect the people against outrages.

Question. Without any regard to whether they were perpetrated by democrats or republicans?

Answer. Yes, sir, I do not think that would make any difference; that is, that is my impression, while I do not know that is so; that was the general understanding in the community.

Question. So far as you had any understanding or information, was it to act upon elections in any shape or form?

Answer. No, sir, I never heard it said it was to have anything to do with elections.

By Mr. Van Trump:

Question. In Tennessee you did not care much about elections then?

Answer. A large portion of the people in the State were disfranchised, and they did not attempt to make any effort to carry elections. . . .

Question. Had it any limitations as to membership?

Answer. I cannot tell you that, for I was never in the organization but once or twice. I went there more to see what was going on than anything else, and paid very little attention to it.

Question. Did they admit boys into the order?

Answer. I do not think they did.

Question. Did they admit negroes?

Answer. I do not think they did.

Question. Did they admit women?

Answer. I do not think they did.

Question. It was an organization of white men?

Answer. I think so.

Question. And from that they called it Pale Faces?

Answer. Yes, sir. . . .

Question. About this order of Pale Faces; you understand that to be a secret order?

Answer. Yes, sir; just as Odd Fellowship and Masonry would be, and I presume the Loyal League was.

Question. So when I asked you if you belonged to the Knights of the White Camelia, and you said you did, you at first thought I was referring to the Pale Faces?

Answer. Yes, sir.

Question. The principles were about the same?

Answer. I do not know what the White Camelia's were.

Question. It professed to be an order for the protection of white people against disorders, particularly by the blacks.

Answer. The great fear of the people at that time was that they would be dragged into a revolution something like San Domingo.[1]

Question. A war of races?

Answer. Yes; a war of races. The object of the people was not to disobey the laws of the country, but to see them enforced and to fortify themselves against anything of the sort. That was my understanding of all these things.

Question. Of all these orders, Ku-Klux, Pale Faces, Knights of the White Camelia?

Answer. No, sir; I do not know anything about the Knights of the White Camelia; I never heard of them before. The object of the organization was to prevent a general slaughter of women and children, and to prepare themselves to resist anything of the kind.

Question. Was not that same apprehension broadcast all over the South, so far as your being in fear of a negro insurrection or a war of races?

Answer. I think it was. During the war our servants remained with us, and behaved very well. When the war was over our servants began to mix with the republicans, and they broke off from the Southern people, and were sulky and insolent. There was a general fear throughout the country that there would be an uprising, and that with those men who had stopped among us—those men who came in among us, came there and went to our kitchens and consulted with the negroes—many of them never came about the houses at all. It was different with me. I carried seven Federal officers home with me, after the war was over, and I rented them plantations, some of my own lands, and some of my neighbors'. In 1866 those seven officers made a crop in my neighborhood. I assisted those men, and found great relief from them. They got me my hands, and they kept my hands engaged for me.

Question. The negroes had confidence in them because they were Northern men?

Answer. Yes, sir. I persuaded our people to pursue the same course. These men were all young men, and they made my house their home on Sundays.

Question. It seems you had more confidence in Northern men than others down there had?

Answer. I think I had.

---

[1]A slave revolt in the French-controlled colony (1791–1804), which culminated in the elimination of slavery there and the founding of the Republic of Haiti.

Question. You say there was a general feeling all through the South, at least there was in Tennessee, of apprehension of general trouble with the negroes, out of which grew this organization?

Answer. That was the cause of it. . . .

By Mr. COBURN:

Question. You have said something about a war of races being apprehended. Had you any more reason to apprehend a war of races after the rebellion was over than during the rebellion?

Answer. A great deal more.

Question. Why was that?

Answer. For the reason that during the war the negroes remained at home working and were quiet, and were not organized. After the war, they left their homes, traveled all over the country, killed all the stock there was in the country to eat, were holding these night meetings, were carrying arms, and were making threats.

Question. Is not the negro naturally submissive and quiet?

Answer. Generally so.

Question. Were they suffering from the hands of the white men as many wrongs after the war as before and during the war?

Answer. I think more; I do not think they were suffering any during the war.

Question. What wrongs?

Answer. They were dissatisfied and disposed to fight and be abusive. They would kill stock, and when arrested large crowds of them would gather around the magistrates' offices, and threaten to take them away, and they did in several instances; and they had fights.

Question. You say there was a general apprehension throughout the whole country that there would be a war of races?

Answer. I think so; there was great fear.

Question. What class of men organized to prevent this war of races; were they rowdies and rough men?

Answer. No, sir; worthy men who belonged to the southern army; the others were not to be trusted; they would not fight when the war was on them, and of course they would not do anything when it was over.

Question. Do you think that had any effect throughout the South to prevent a war of races?

Answer. I think the organizing of these men, and showing a disposition that we were prepared to resist it, prevented it.

Question. You think the negroes understood that to be the fact, that there was an organization throughout the South of that kind?

Answer. I think so.

Question. And hence they behaved themselves better?

Answer. I think so; I know one man in Maury County told me that he had lost nearly everything that he had; that the pike that passed his house used to be lined from dark till daylight with negroes traveling forward; that these men traveled up the road one night, about twenty of them, in disguise; that it had been a month since those men had passed up the road, and he had not seen a negro there at night since then.

Question. Were there no lawless white men who went around robbing?

Answer. I think so, and on the negroes' credit, too.

Question. By what means did these "Pale Faces" expect to prevent these disorders?

Answer. By organizing themselves and holding themselves in readiness to resist anything of that sort that did occur.

Question. By what means?

Answer. Of course they had but one way to resist; they did not expect any assistance from the government of the State of Tennessee.

Question. Prevent it by punishing the offenders?

Answer. And defending themselves.

Question. Suppose an outrage was committed and they caught the offender, what would they do?

Answer. There was more or less mob law about that time through the Southern States.

Question. The object was to resist outlawry and punish offenders?

Answer. Yes, sir; I do not think the people intended to go and violate or wrong any one; but it was to punish those men who were guilty, and who the law would not touch; and to defend themselves in case of an attack.

Question. What reason have you to believe that they have disbanded?

Answer. From the fact that I do not hear anything of them, and it was generally understood that they were to be disbanded; it was generally understood throughout the country I have been in that they have disbanded, that there was no organization, and nothing in that line, except amongst lawless men—men who were trying to do something they ought not to do, to violate the law.

24

A. S. LAKIN

Washington, D.C.

June 13, 1871

Reverend A. S. Lakin, of the Methodist Episcopal Church in Alabama, testified before the committee in Washington, D.C. During his testimony, he discussed his travels throughout the state and tried to explain why and how the Ku Klux Klan spread and was welcomed by southerners.

Rev. A. S. LAKIN sworn and examined.

By the CHAIRMAN:

Question. In what part of Alabama do you reside, and how long have you resided there?

Answer. I reside in Huntsville, in the northern part of Alabama; I have resided there five years and about eight months.

Question. What is your profession?

Answer. I am a minister of the gospel.

Question. Of what denomination?

Answer. Of the Methodist Episcopal church.

Question. Will you now proceed to give us your knowledge and observation of the organization and operations of what is known as the Ku-Klux Klan in Alabama during your residence there? Give us as succinct a statement as you can of such occurrences as have fallen under your own observation.

Answer. In the fall of 1867 I was appointed to the Montgomery district.

Question. As a preacher or as presiding elder?

Answer. As presiding elder. We were then a missionary conference; but our reports were obstructed, our drafts were abstracted, and our preachers were in suffering circumstances. I was ordered by Bishop Clark to go out on a roving commission, with the names and amounts due each presiding elder and each preacher in each of the presiding elder districts. The drafts were forwarded to me and I cashed them, and, in my saddle, I traveled six hundred and fifty miles, through the mountains and valleys, permeating almost every portion of Northern Alabama. In my travels I put up with some of the leading men of the State, and learned from them this fact: that they never would submit; that they never would yield; they had lost their property, their reputation; and, last and worst of all their sufferings, their slaves were made their equals, or were likely to be, and perhaps their superiors, to rule over them. In extended conversations with them I inquired how we would help ourselves. They said there was an organization already very extensive, and that would spread over the Southern States, that would rid them of this terrible calamity. I stated that we would be arrested and punished; that the Government would visit upon us probably heavier judgments than any we had experienced. They said they could rule that and control it. I asked how, and they replied, "Why, suppose a man drops out here"—meaning that they would kill him—"while that is being investigated, another will drop out here and there and yonder, until the cases are so frequent and numerous that we will overwhelm the courts, and nothing can withstand the omnipotence of popular sentiment and public opinion." I gathered these facts from various sources; they seemed to be patent. On my arrival at Huntsville, after this long and tedious tour, I learned of the organization of the Ku-Klux Klan. It answered precisely the description, and seemed to answer precisely the design expressed by these leading men.

25

WILLIAM M. LOWE

Huntsville, Alabama

October 13, 1871

William Lowe, a white lawyer born and raised in Huntsville, Alabama, who served in the Confederate army and was later elected to the Alabama and U.S. House of Representatives, was called before the committee by the minority. During his testimony, he provided information about why he believed the Ku Klux Klan was organized, arguing that the group maintained law and order and mirrored the old slave patrols that existed before the Civil War.

WILLIAM M. LOWE sworn and examined.

The CHAIRMAN. As this witness has been called at the request of the minority, his examination may be conducted by General Blair.

By Mr. BLAIR:

Question. State your present place of residence, Colonel.
Answer. I was born and raised, and still live, in Huntsville, Alabama.
Question. What is your age?
Answer. I will be thirty the 16th of next January.
Question. What is your business or profession?
Answer. Lawyer.
Question. Do you practice law here?
Answer. Yes, sir; I practice law here and in this judicial circuit, and occasionally in Limestone, the adjoining county.
Question. What counties compose this judicial circuit?
Answer. Madison, Marshall, Johnson, De Kalb, Cherokee, Blount, and I also practice occasionally in Limestone, which is not in this circuit.
Question. Were you at any time the solicitor for this district?
Answer. I was. I was elected solicitor in 1865 under the Patton government.[1]

By Mr. BUCKLEY:

Question. By the legislature?
Answer. By the legislature. . . .
Question. Was there anything in the condition of society, in the disorganization which followed the war, and the casting adrift upon society of the soldiers, and the turning loose of the negroes from their former masters, to excite apprehension and serve as a pretext for this organization [the Ku Klux Klan]?
Answer. Yes, sir; I thought so. I do not think that the Ku-Klux Klan was any remedy for these evils. Indeed, we could see that the negroes, being suddenly liberated, showed in all their conduct a bearing that they mistook license for liberty; they would come to political meetings with their arms; they would sometimes get drunk and you would

---

[1]Robert M. Patton was governor of Alabama, 1865–1867.

see occasional instances of their returning home firing their arms
off at night; using threatening language towards the whites, towards
"rebels" and "democrats." Well, the rebels and democrats included
the whole body of the white people of the country, and the people
who lived in the country away from the little towns—white families
of two or three, surrounded by hundreds of negroes—were appre-
hensive. After a great civil convulsion, such as ours was, the laws
were not enforced as they had been. The whole foundations of society were broken up; that was the excuse given for the organization of
the Ku-Klux Klan. I regarded it then, as I regard it now, as possibly
a temporary remedy for these evils, but it was very much like quack
medicine—while it would cure the special disease it would infect the
body politic and injure the whole constitution. I was a member of the
democratic State committee, chairman of the democratic congressional committee, and chairman of the democratic county committee, and I know that the sentiment of the leaders of the democratic
party—of the democratic politicians throughout the State—was
hostile to the organization of the Ku-Klux Klan.

Question. I observe, Colonel Lowe, in the dispatches that come to us
now detailing the awful calamity which has just fallen upon the city of
Chicago, that in the midst of this distress there were some persons
who gave themselves up to robbery and plunder, and that the people
have taken the law into their own hands and put them to death. Was
there any similitude in the case of which we are now speaking after
all the disorganization of the war and the calamities which had fallen
upon this country, and in the silence of the laws and inefficiency of
their officers—was there some excuse, or a similar excuse, for these
attempts to preserve order in that case to which I have alluded?

Answer. I think so, sir. The justification or excuse which was given for
the organization of the Ku-Klux Klan was, that it was essential to preserve society; they thought after such a civil convulsion as we had had
in this country, the feebleness with which the laws were executed,
the disturbed state of society, it was necessary that there should be
some patrol of the sort, especially for the country districts outside of
town; that it had been a legal and recognized mode of preserving the
peace and keeping order in the former condition of these States.

Question. The patrol?

Answer. Yes, sir.

Question. The patrol had been a recognized legal method of preserving
the peace?

Answer. Yes, sir.

Question. And it was, therefore, natural that it should be resumed?
Answer. Yes, sir.

Committee Conclusions

26

Minority Report
February 19, 1872

The minority report of the congressional committee, submitted by Mis-
souri's Democratic senator Frank P. Blair and signed by the other
Democrats on the committee, minimized the voluminous evidence of
violence and lawlessness the committee gathered during its interviews.
Instead, the report concentrated on alleged deficiencies of the Republican
governments in the South and the supposed attempts by carpetbaggers and
scalawags—white Republicans who moved to the South from the North
(with their possessions in carpetbags) and white Republicans native to
the South, respectively—to exploit black voters. These two groups helped
African Americans create a Republican coalition in many areas of the
region. The report painted a dire picture of the disastrous results of black
suffrage and political activity, particularly in South Carolina, and sig-
nificantly influenced later historical writing on Reconstruction.

The majority of the Committee on Alleged Outrages in the Southern
States having resolved to make their report to the two Houses of Congress before the testimony taken by the sub-committees sent to those
States has been printed, and having sent their report to the Public
Printer without giving the undersigned opportunity properly to ascertain its contents, or the conclusoins [*sic*] of the majority, it becomes necessary that the undersigned, members of the committee, should submit
their views of the testimony which has been taken, and of all the matters
committed to their charge.

KKK Testimony, 1:289–588.

The evidence taken in Georgia and Florida and in Alabama and Mississippi, cover many of the transactions touched in the testimony previously taken, and no one can form any just opinion of those transactions without reading all the testimony as well that which was taken by the sub-committees visiting the States named, as that which was taken before the committee in Washington, and yet the majority of the committee have chosen to make their report without waiting to have the whole testimony printed, and we are compelled to believe that they have come to their conclusions upon partial, imperfect, and prejudiced statements, furnished by witnesses examined in Washington, who were refuted, and, in many instances, shown to be utterly unworthy of belief, by the testimony of their neighbors who subsequently testified before the sub-committees.

As these witnesses testified as to the most important matters which have been laid to the charge of the white people of the South, it is possible that their testimony may be paraded by the majority of the committee, and relied upon as throwing upon them the responsibility of the disorders which have unhappily afflicted these States. It will be necessary, therefore, to expose these men, so that no one can be deceived who desires to know the truth, and to show also the character of this proceeding by which whole communities are sought to be calumniated and defamed for political objects. The atrocious measures by which millions of white people have been put at the mercy of the semi-barbarous negroes of the South, and the vilest of the white people, both from the North and South, who have been constituted the leaders of this black horde, are now sought to be justified and defended by defaming the people upon whom this unspeakable outrage had been committed. . . .

. . . We shall show by the strongest testimony that this state of things is the clearest natural offspring of as corrupt and oppressive a system of local State government as ever disgraced humanity, and utterly unparalleled in the history of civilization. No modern instance of wrong and oppression, of robbery and usurpation, can approach it in wickedness and infamy; nor can any people on the face of the globe, not even the unhappy Poles[1] in their darkest days of suffering, rival the great body of the best citizens of South Carolina, for the patient, we had almost said the abject, forbearance with which they have submitted to the infernal persecution of their rulers. That class described so aptly by the Herald's[2] correspondent did not submit to it; but who will deny the proposition

---

[1] A person of Polish descent.
[2] Daily newspaper published in New York City from 1835 to 1924.

that while we denounce the effect, we should also condemn the cause? That while we punish the crime we should also remedy the evil which produces the crime? It is an axiomatic truth that bad government will produce bad men among the best people on earth; and that has clearly been the cause of Ku-Kluxism in South Carolina. . . . The minority member of the sub-committee deemed it only a waste of time even to attempt to hunt up countervailing testimony as to the commission of these outrages, though he by no means admits them to the extravagant extent as claimed; he felt that the truth of history would be better vindicated, and that a knowledge of the means would be more successfully furnished to the national legislature, to apply, if so disposed, the true remedy for this great evil, by showing the *cause* and the *process* of robbery, corruption, and outrage which have produced it. These two classes of people, white and black, are, from the necessity of their position, constantly brought into close and sharp contact with each other. They are fierce competitors in the earning of their daily bread; they are competitors in labor in all its varied rural forms, and in the renting of what is now called one and two horse cotton farms; for there exist no longer in South Carolina any great proprietary cotton plantations, at least in that portion of it visited by the committee. The antagonism, therefore, which exists between these two classes of the population of South Carolina does not spring from any political cause, in the ordinary party sense of the term; but it grows out of that instinctive and irrepressible repugnance to compulsory affiliation with another race, planted by the God of nature in the breast of the white man, perhaps more strongly manifested in the uneducated portion of a people, and aggravated and intensified by the fact that the negro has been placed as a *ruler* over him. This is not the place to discuss negro suffrage or negro equality, even in a government or State where the negro is in a controlling majority; but we cannot refrain from declaring right here that no fair-minded man, we care not what may be his prejudices or his party ties, can go down to South Carolina and see the practical workings of the system there without being driven to the admission that the policy which has made a San Domingo of one of the States of this Union is one of the most terrible blunders ever committed, one of the most reckless and unwise political movements ever inaugurated in a government of fixed laws and constitutions.

As we have just remarked, we do not propose to discuss at large the question of negro government in these pages; but we feel that it would be a dereliction of duty on our part if, after what we have witnessed in South Carolina, we did not admonish the American people that the present condition of things in the South cannot last. It was an oft-quoted political apothegm, long prior to the war, that no government could exist "half slave and half free." The paraphrase of that proposition is equally true, that no government can long exist "half black and half white." If the republican party, or its all-powerful leaders in the North, cannot see this, if they are so absorbed in the idea of this newly discovered political divinity in the negro, that they cannot comprehend its social repugnance or its political dangers; or, knowing it, have the wanton, wicked, and criminal purpose of disregarding its consequences, whether in the present or in the future, and the great mass of American white citizens should still be so mad as to sustain them in their heedless career of forcing negro supremacy over white men, why then "farewell, a long farewell," to constitutional liberty on this continent, and the glorious form of government bequeathed to us by our fathers. . . .

Who would have dreamed, fifteen years ago, what highest and most far-seeing intellect among the great men who established this Government upon the basis of homogeneity of race and color, could have imagined that in the first century of its existence African freedmen, of the lowest type of ignorance and brutality, would rule a sovereign State of the Union, and be the arbiters of the rights and property of a race who have ruled the destinies of nations ever since government was known among men? Such a state of things may last so long as the party shall last which had the power and audacity to inaugurate it, and no longer. But whenever that party shall go down, as go down it will at some time not long in the future, that will be the end of the political power of the negro among white men on this continent. Men in the phrensy [frenzy] of political passions may shut their eyes to this fact now, but it will come at any time when the negro shall cease to be a party necessity in the politics of this country. Thousands of republicans, even now, hate him for his insolence and for his arrogance in the ready self-assertion of his new-found rights and privileges. The truly sincere and rational humanitarian looks with sorrow upon the future status of the poor, deluded negro; for in the near state of things which is to come, when the two great parties which now exist shall have passed away, he sees either the exodus or the extinction of this disturbing element in the social and political condition of the more powerful race.

> "O that a man might know
> The end of this day's business ere it come!
> But it sufficeth *that the day will end,*
> And then the end is known."

The condition of things in South Carolina, we dare assert, is without a parallel in the history of any people of any civilization. . . .

. . . Barbaric vengeance never went so far, never so violated the natural fitness of things, as to place the slave over his former master, the arbiter of that master's rights, by way of retribution for his former servitude, even where master and slave were of the same race, or at least of the same color. . . .

The first prominent cause of public disturbance, of which these carpet-bag patriots were the authors, was a most thorough and secret organization of the negroes, in all the counties of the State, into Loyal Leagues, in many instances armed and adopting all the formula of signs, pass-words, and grips, of an oath-bound secret organization. Who does not know, who has any knowledge at all of the negro's nature, that in an organization like this, headed by dishonest and unscrupulous white men, that the negro would be a mere blind and dumb machine in their hands? That has been its operation in South Carolina. At Spartanburgh, one of the members of the sub-committee inquired of a negro witness, on the stand, how it was that there was no difference of opinion among the negroes upon political questions, like among the whites, and why it was that they all voted the republican ticket. His reply was, *"Why Lor' bress your soul, massa, we swo' to do dat in de League!"* That simple answer by this newly created suffragist, this mere automaton of the ballot, is a full explanation of the political solidity of the negro race in South Carolina. The dumb mule on whose back he vain-gloriously rides to the polls might just as well vote as his rider, under such circumstances, for there would be scarcely any less volition in the act of the mule than there would be on the part of the negro, at least such as we find him in South Carolina. . . .

. . . Will any one doubt, who has personally witnessed its practical working, that negro suffrage and negro government in South Carolina is a hopeless and total failure? Its institution was not only a political crime, but worse than that; it was a most unequivocal and eggregious [*sic*] political blunder, as it must ever be where the negroes are in the majority. Pseudo philanthropists may talk never so loud and eloquently about an "equality before the law," where equality is not found in the great natural law of race ordained by the Creator. That cannot be changed by statute which has been irrevocably fixed by the fiat of the Almighty. Wherever the two races exist coequally by compulsory legislation, antagonism will exist also. There can be no peace or harmony in such a condition of political organization, especially when the natural repulsion is intensified by the teachings of recreant portions of the opposite race. It will not be forgotten how these teachings occurred, even in the times of slavery. It is some explanation, outside of the action of the carpet-baggers, of the hostile feeling entertained by the negroes of South Carolina against the white population, that the few most intelligent and influential among them, who in times of slavery were taught to read either by their masters or their masters' children, had their minds poisoned by incendiary publications distributed among them by the old anti-slavery party in the North. That class, however limited in numbers, have been the ready emissaries of the carpet-baggers, to sow hatred and vengeance in the minds of the great mass of the negro population. The sudden transition from slavery to freedom, their unexpected investiture with political power and social importance in their new relations, the tenure of office which they could not comprehend, naturally made them jealous of their former masters, and to look upon them with distrust and antipathy. They had been taught to believe that, if ever these new rights were wrested from them, it would be done by those who once held them in servitude. But while the negroes of the South have position and power in the administration of public affairs now, who can say, who can look into the future so clearly as to enable him to say, how long this unnatural state of things will last. . . .

The Loyal Leagues were organized in 1867, long before Ku-Kluxism reared its lawless head in South Carolina. In the convention of 1868, which adopted a State constitution under the dictates of Congress, the operations of this oath-bound League were clearly manifested. The convention was composed of one hundred and twenty-one members, seventy-two of whom were negroes and forty-nine were white men. Of the seventy-two negro members, fifty-nine paid no taxes, and were not returned on the tax-books. . . .

It will be observed that this riot at Yorkville, although nothing serious accrued, . . . like the other riots of like character, was caused by the arming of the negroes, and their insolent and outrageous conduct after being armed. The uniformity in the conduct of the negroes, after they were organized and armed, shows very conclusively that they well understood the object of their being thus armed by the governor to the exclusion of the white men. It must be a matter of wonder to any one who has any just conception of the state of affairs in South Carolina, that a fierce and bloody war of races was avoided under the circumstances. . . .

When is this fell [bitter, sour] spirit of political vengeance against millions of free-born citizens to end? Is it safe, to say nothing of its injustice, much longer to continue this scheme of party persecutions? Is peace so assured among the nations of the earth that we have nothing more to fear from the chances of war? Are there no signs for the future, no portentious [*sic*] clouds in the far-off horizon, betokening storm and tempest, to give warning to those who have in charge the ship of state? Ay, omens are even now in the sky! . . .

FRANK P. BLAIR.
T. F. BAYARD.
S. S. COX.
JAMES B. BECK.
P. VAN TRUMP.
A. M. WADDELL.
J. C. ROBINSON.
J. M. HANKS.

27

Majority Report
February 19, 1872

The majority report of the congressional committee, submitted by Vermont's Republican representative Luke P. Poland and signed by the other Republican members of the committee, used the evidence collected during the months of testimony to confirm the existence of lawlessness and violence throughout the former Confederacy. Moreover, the report contends that Congress was correct in passing the third Enforcement Act before the committee began its work.

The proceedings and debates in Congress show that, whatever other causes were assigned for disorders in the late insurrectionary States, the execution of the laws and the security of life and property were alleged to be most seriously threatened by the existence and acts of organized bands of armed and disguised men, known as Ku-Klux.

Inquiring, as our primary duty, into the truth of these allegations, in those States where such acts have most recently been committed, the investigation necessarily assumed a wider range. Not only has inquiry been made as to the commission of outrages, as to the execution of the laws by the superior courts and inferior magistrates, but bad legislation, official incompetency, corruption, and other causes, having been assigned as accounting for, if not justifying disorders, they, too, have, to a large extent, entered into the statements and opinions of witnesses.

There is a remarkable concurrence of testimony to the effect that, in those of the late rebellious States into whose condition we have examined, the courts and juries administer justice between man and man in all ordinary cases, civil and criminal; and while there is this concurrence on this point, the evidence is equally decisive that redress cannot be obtained against those who commit crimes in disguise and at night. The reasons assigned are that identification is difficult, almost impossible; that when this is attempted, the combinations and oaths of the order come in and release the culprit by perjury either upon the witness-stand or in the jury-box; and that the terror inspired by their acts, as well as the public sentiment in their favor in many localities, paralyzes the arm of civil power. . . .

The race so recently emancipated, against which banishment or serfdom is thus decreed, but which has been clothed by the Government with the rights and responsibilities of citizenship, ought not to be, and we feel assured will not be left hereafter without protection against the hostilities and sufferings it has endured in the past, as long as the legal and constitutional powers of the Government are adequate to afford it. Communities suffering such evils and influenced by such extreme feelings may be slow to learn that relief can come only from a ready obedience to and support of constituted authority, looking to the modes provided by law for redress of all grievances. That Southern communities do not seem to yield this ready obedience at once should not deter the friends of good government in both sections from hoping and working for that end.

Northern communities, exasperated by the delay and insubordination, may be reminded that the elements of the two societies are widely different. Composed of those who, a few years since, ruled the State and exacted obedience to their will from their slaves, and held absolute sway over the votes of their white dependents, but who are now reduced in influence and in wealth by the events of war; of the poor white who has found himself, as he supposes, degraded by the elevation of the negro to political equality with him, his vote before having been the chief badge of his superiority; of the negro, not only voting, but ruling the State, in office with or over his former master, or struggling with the evils of poverty in beginning life for himself after the best years of his strength have been spent in the service of others—all these elements beget feelings and result in disorders to which northern communities are strangers.

The strong feeling which led to rebellion and sustained brave men, however mistaken, in resisting the Government which demanded their submission to its authority, the sincerity of whose belief was attested by their enormous sacrifice of life and treasure—this feeling cannot be expected to subside at once, nor in years. It required full forty years to develop disaffection into sedition, and sedition into treason. Should we not be patient if in less than ten we have a fair prospect of seeing so many who were armed enemies becoming obedient citizens? Should we not give all encouragement to those who manifest the disposition now to become such, especially when it is apparent, as it is, that in many sections well-disposed men were deterred by fear of the power of an armed and desperate conspiracy from affording aid to the authorities in enforcing the law? But while we invoke this forbearance and conciliation, fully recognizing that from far the largest part of the southern people a reluctant obedience is all that is to be hoped for, let it be understood that less than obedience the Government cannot accept. Obedient citizens they cannot be considered who themselves, complaining of bad laws, excuse or encourage the masked and armed mobs that override all law. Brave and magnanimous enemies even they cannot be reckoned who permit the remnants of rebellious feeling, the antagonisms of race, or the bitterness of political partisanships to degrade the soldiers of [General Robert E.] Lee and [General Albert Sidney] Johnston into the cowardly midnight prowlers and assassins who scourge and kill the poor and defenseless.

Against all such crimes, as well as against incompetency and corruption in office, the power of an intelligent public sentiment and of the courts of justice should be invoked and united; and appealing for patience and forbearance in the North while time and these powers are doing their work, we would also appeal to the good sense of Southern men, if they sincerely desire to accomplish political reforms through a change in the negro vote. If their theory is true that he votes solidly now with the republican party, and is kept there by his ignorance and by deception, all that is necessary to keep him there is to keep up by their countenance the Ku-Klux organization.

Having the rights of a citizen and a voter, neither of those rights can be abrogated by whipping him. If his political opinions are erroneous he will not take kindly to the opposite creed when its apostles come to inflict the scourge upon himself, and outrage upon his wife and children. If he is ignorant, he will not be educated by burning his schoolhouses and exiling his teachers; if he is wicked, he will not be made better by banishing to Liberia his religious teachers. If the resuscitation of the State is desired by his labor, neither will be secured by a persecution which depopulates townships and prevents the introduction of new labor and of capital.

The law of 1871 has been effective in suppressing for the present, to a great extent, the operations of masked and disguised men in North and South Carolina. Bills have also been found by grand juries in Georgia, Alabama, and Mississippi, but comparatively few, if any, of the defendants in the last-named States have yet been tried. The apparent cessation of operations should not lead to a conclusion that community would be safe if protective measures were withdrawn. These should be continued until there remains no further doubt of the actual suppression and disarming of this wide-spread and dangerous conspiracy.

The results of suspending the writ of *habeas corpus* in South Carolina show that where the membership, mysteries, and power of the organization have been kept concealed this is the most and perhaps only effective remedy for its suppression; and in view of its cessation and resumption of hostilities at different times, of its extent and power, and that in several of the States where it exists the courts have not yet held terms at which the cases can be tried, we recommend that the power conferred on the President by the fourth section of that act be extended until the end of the next session of Congress.

In view also of the large number of indictments found in the several courts under this act which yet remain untried, and of the evident encouragement derived from the belief that the present United States courts cannot possibly reach and try them within any reasonable time, we recommend such an increase of the judiciary of the United States by districts and circuits in the States shown to be affected by these disorders as, in the judgment of Congress, will secure speedy and certain justice to be administered, and leave no hope of impunity to criminals by the law's delay.

The continuance of disabilities is the only cause not yet considered. No man under disabilities has avowed himself as either committing or encouraging outrages for that reason, and no member of the organization has justified their acts upon that ground. It is one of the pretexts made by those who were willing to urge any plausible excuse for outrages which admit of none. But to remove alleged impediments to the local government encountered by the existence of disabilities to hold office, and being satisfied that there should be a general removal of them, with proper conditions and exceptions, we recommend the passage of a law for that purpose, agreeing in the recommendation made by the President to exclude from its benefits "any great criminals distinguished above all others for the part they took in opposition to the Government."

In this connection we wish to say that, as disregard of law has been the evil so largely complained of and so widely extended in the late insurrectionary States, no encouragement should be given to those who have accepted office in defiance of the existence of these constitutional disabilities, or elected to office men whom they knew to be excluded by them.

JOHN SCOTT, *Chairman.*
Z. CHANDLER,
BENJ. F. RICE,
JOHN POOL,
DANIEL D. PRATT,
On the part of the Senate.

LUKE P. POLAND, *Chairman.*
HORACE MAYNARD,
GLENNI W. SCOFIELD,
JOHN F. FARNSWORTH,
JOHN COBURN,
JOB E. STEVENSON,
BENJ. F. BUTLER,
WILLIAM E. LANSING,
On the part of the House of Representatives.

A Brief Chronology of Reconstruction and the Ku Klux Klan Hearings (1863–1877)

1863 President Abraham Lincoln issues the Proclamation of Amnesty and Reconstruction, also called the Ten Percent Plan.

1864 Congress passes the Wade-Davis Reconstruction bill; Lincoln refuses to sign it into law.

1865 General Robert E. Lee surrenders at Appomattox Court House, Virginia.

Lincoln assassinated.

President Andrew Johnson pardons nearly all white southerners who pledge allegiance to the Union; Presidential Reconstruction begins.

All the former Confederate states except Texas reorganize under Johnson's Reconstruction plan.

Thirteenth Amendment ratified.

Congress establishes the Joint Committee on Reconstruction.

1866 Ku Klux Klan founded in Tennessee.

1867 Congress takes over Reconstruction; Radical Reconstruction (or Congressional Reconstruction) begins.

First, second, and third Reconstruction Acts passed, all over Johnson's veto.

1868 Fourteenth Amendment ratified.

Ulysses S. Grant elected president.

1870 Hiram R. Revels of Mississippi becomes first African American elected to the U.S. Senate.

Congress passes the first Enforcement Act.

Fifteenth Amendment ratified.

President Grant discusses violence in the South in a special message to Congress and asks Congress to investigate the matter.

Joseph H. Rainey of South Carolina becomes the first black member of the U.S. House of Representatives.

1871   Congress passes the second (February) and third (April) Enforcement Acts, the latter popularly known as the Ku Klux Klan Act.

Congress forms the Joint Select Committee to Inquire into the Condition of Affairs in the Late Insurrectionary States.

Arrests and prosecutions of suspected Klansmen begin and continue into 1872.

Ku Klux Klan hearings conclude.

1872   Congressional committee submits its findings, which include the majority and minority reports, accompanied by thirteen volumes of testimony.

Ulysses S. Grant reelected.

1873   Colfax massacre in Louisiana.

1875   Congress passes the Civil Rights Act of 1875.

Blanche Kelso Bruce, a former slave, elected U.S. senator in Mississippi; becomes first African American to serve a full term.

1876   Hamburg massacre in South Carolina.

Rutherford B. Hayes elected president.

1877   Compromise of 1877 ends Reconstruction.

Questions for Consideration

1. As a historical source, what do the Ku Klux Klan hearings reveal about the social, economic, political, and legal status of blacks during Reconstruction? To what extent did vigilante violence and intimidation affect southern African Americans' status in the postwar era?

2. Describe the actions and motives that witnesses attributed to the Ku Klux Klan. In what ways do the descriptions differ between regions? In what ways do they differ based on race or gender?

3. Based on the testimony, what was the purpose and organization of groups like the Ku Klux Klan in the years immediately after the Civil War?

4. Judging from the testimony, how did African Americans define freedom after the Civil War? What limits did whites try to impose on that freedom?

5. What do the hearings tell a student of Reconstruction about the displacement caused by the pervasive violence during this period?

6. Night riders used various types of violence and methods of intimidation during Reconstruction. What difference did their targets' gender make in their modes of attack?

7. What effect did postwar violence in the South have on black children?

8. What was the purpose of the hearings? Who had access to the findings of the hearings? How might the various audiences—southerners and northerners, men and women, whites and African Americans—have interpreted the testimony differently? Did the testimony and the findings of the committee affect actual conditions on the ground? Why or why not? If so, how?

9. Though the hearings had the appearance of legal proceedings, the committee allowed hearsay evidence to be included in the recorded testimony. This ran counter to traditional legal restrictions on the acceptance of hearsay testimony. Why would the committee have chosen to ignore these restrictions? Did the acceptance of hearsay change the legitimacy of the hearings? Why or why not? If so, how?

10. What patterns can you identify in the ways in which Republicans and Democrats interacted with the witnesses? Does it seem as though the members of the committee were looking for evidence to support their own notions about the violence in the South or seeking to discover the truth behind it? Explain.

11. What were the limits of federal power during Reconstruction, and how is this demonstrated in the testimony?

12. What do the firsthand accounts of violence tell us about the trauma African Americans suffered in the post-emancipation period?

13. How did white southerners justify the acts of violence they were accused of committing or that took place in their particular regions?

14. Are there limitations to these hearings as a historical source? What are the advantages and disadvantages of using this testimony to understand the post-emancipation South?

15. Why should students of history be interested in studying the Ku Klux Klan hearings?

Selected Bibliography

Baker, Bruce E. *What Reconstruction Meant: Historical Memory in the American South*. Charlottesville: University of Virginia Press, 2007.

Bercaw, Nancy. *Gendered Freedoms: Race, Rights, and the Politics of Household in the Delta, 1861–1875*. Gainesville: University Press of Florida, 2003.

Blight, David William. *Race and Reunion: The Civil War in American Memory*. Cambridge, Mass.: Harvard University Press, 2001.

Brown, Thomas J. *Reconstructions: New Perspectives on the Postbellum United States*. New York: Oxford University Press, 2006.

Budiansky, Stephen. *The Bloody Shirt: Terror after Appomattox*. New York: Viking, 2008.

Clinton, Catherine. "Bloody Terrain: Freedwomen, Sexuality, and Violence during Reconstruction." *Georgia Historical Quarterly* 76 (1992): 313–32.

Davis, Hugh. *We Will Be Satisfied with Nothing Less: The African American Struggle for Equal Rights in the North during Reconstruction*. Ithaca, N.Y.: Cornell University Press, 2011.

Dixon, Thomas. *The Clansman: An Historical Romance of the Ku Klux Klan*. New York: Doubleday, 1905.

Du Bois, W. E. B. *Black Reconstruction: An Essay toward a History of the Part Which Black Folk Played in the Attempt to Reconstruct Democracy in America, 1860–1890*. 1935. Reprint, Millwood, N.Y.: Kraus-Thomson, 1976.

Edwards, Laura F. *Gendered Strife and Confusion: The Political Culture of Reconstruction*. Urbana-Champaign: University of Illinois Press, 1997.

Emberton, Carole. *Beyond Redemption: Race, Violence, and the American South after the Civil War*. Chicago: University of Chicago Press, 2013.

———. "Testimony before the Joint Committee on Reconstruction Atrocities in the South against Blacks." In *Milestone Documents in African American History*, 633–49. Dallas: Schlager, 2010.

Faulkner, Carol. *Women's Radical Reconstruction: The Freedmen's Aid Movement*. Philadelphia: University of Pennsylvania Press, 2004.

Fishel, Leslie H., Jr. "The North and the Negro, 1865–1900." Ph.D. diss., Harvard University, 1953.

Fitzgerald, Michael W. "Extralegal Violence and the Planter Class: The Ku Klux Klan in the Alabama Black Belt during Reconstruction." In *Local Matters: Race, Crime, and Justice in the Nineteenth Century South*, edited by Christopher Waldrep and Donald G. Nieman. Athens: University of Georgia Press, 2001.

———. "The Ku Klux Klan: Property Crime and the Plantation System in Reconstruction Alabama." *Agricultural History* 71, no. 2 (1997): 186–206.

———. *Splendid Failure: Postwar Reconstruction in the American South.* Chicago: Ivan R. Dee, 2007.

———. *The Union League Movement in the Deep South: Politics and Agricultural Change during Reconstruction.* Baton Rouge: Louisiana State University Press, 1989.

Foner, Eric. *Reconstruction: America's Unfinished Revolution, 1863–1877.* New York: Harper & Row, 1988.

Franklin, John Hope. *The Militant South, 1800–1861.* Cambridge, Mass.: Harvard University Press, 1956.

———. *Reconstruction after the Civil War.* Chicago: University of Chicago Press, 1961.

Gillette, William. *Retreat from Reconstruction, 1869–1879.* Baton Rouge: Louisiana State University Press, 1979.

Hahn, Steven. *A Nation under Our Feet: Black Political Struggles in the Rural South, from Slavery to the Great Migration.* Cambridge, Mass.: Harvard University Press, 2003.

Hyman, Harold M., ed. *New Frontiers of the American Reconstruction.* Urbana-Champaign: University of Illinois Press, 1966.

Kantrowitz, Stephen. *Ben Tillman and the Reconstruction of White Supremacy.* Chapel Hill: University of North Carolina Press, 2000.

Keith, LeeAnna. *The Colfax Massacre: The Untold Story of Black Power, White Terror, and the Death of Reconstruction.* New York: Oxford University Press, 2008.

Lemann, Nicholas. *Redemption: The Last Battle of the Civil War.* New York: Farrar, Straus and Giroux, 2006.

Link, William A. *Creating Citizenship in the Nineteenth-Century South.* Gainesville: University Press of Florida, 2013.

Litwack, Leon F. *Been in the Storm So Long: The Aftermath of Slavery.* New York: Knopf, 1979.

Lynch, John R. *Facts of Reconstruction.* New York: Neale, 1913.

McKitrick, Eric L. *Andrew Johnson and Reconstruction.* New York: Oxford University Press, 1988.

Nelson, Scott Reynolds. *Iron Confederacies: Southern Railways, Klan Violence, and Reconstruction.* Chapel Hill: University of North Carolina Press, 1999.

Olsen, Otto H. "The Ku Klux Klan: A Study in Reconstruction Politics and Propaganda." *North Carolina Historical Review* 39 (1962): 340–62.

Parsons, Elaine Frantz. "Midnight Rangers: Costume and Performance in the Reconstruction-Era Ku Klux Klan." *Journal of American History* (2005): 811–36.

Perman, Michael. "Counter Reconstruction: The Role of Violence in Southern Redemption." In *The Facts of Reconstruction: Essays in Honor of John Hope Franklin,* edited by Eric Anderson and Alfred A. Moss Jr., 121–40. Baton Rouge: Louisiana State University Press, 1991.

———. *The Road to Redemption: Southern Politics, 1869–1879.* Chapel Hill: University of North Carolina Press, 1984.

Rable, George C. *But There Was No Peace: The Role of Violence in the Politics of Reconstruction.* Athens: University of Georgia Press, 1984.

Reid, Debra Ann, and Evan P. Bennett. *Beyond Forty Acres and a Mule: African American Landowning Families since Reconstruction.* Gainesville: University Press of Florida, 2012.

Richardson, Heather Cox. *The Death of Reconstruction: Race, Labor, and Politics in the Post–Civil War North, 1865–1901.* Cambridge, Mass.: Harvard University Press, 2001.

———. *West from Appomattox: The Reconstruction of America after the Civil War.* New Haven, Conn.: Yale University Press, 2007.

Rosen, Hannah. *Terror in the Heart of Freedom: Citizenship, Sexual Violence, and the Meaning of Race in the Postemancipation South.* Chapel Hill: University of North Carolina Press, 2008.

Rutherglen, George. *Civil Rights in the Shadow of Slavery: The Constitution, Common Law, and the Civil Rights Act of 1866.* New York: Oxford University Press, 2013.

Schwalm, Leslie A. *A Hard Fight for We: Women's Transition from Slavery to Freedom in South Carolina.* Urbana-Champaign: University of Illinois Press, 1997.

Shapiro, Herbert. "The Ku Klux Klan during Reconstruction: South Carolina Episode." *Journal of Negro History* 49 (1964).

———. *White Violence and Black Response: From Reconstruction to Montgomery.* Amherst: University of Massachusetts Press, 1988.

Silver, Andrew. "Making Minstrelsy of Murder: George Washington Harris, the Ku Klux Klan, and the Reconstruction Aesthetic of Black Fright." *Prospects* 25 (2000): 339–62.

Sinclair, William. *The Aftermath of Slavery: A Study of the Condition and Environment of the American Negro,* edited by Shawn Leigh Alexander. 1905. Reprint, Columbia: University of South Carolina Press, 2012.

Sipress, Joel M. "From the Barrel of a Gun: The Politics of Murder in Grant Parish." *Louisiana History* 42, no. 3 (2001): 303–21.

Smith, John David. *Black Voices from Reconstruction, 1865–1877.* Gainesville: University Press of Florida, 1997.

Sterling, Dorothy. *The Trouble They Seen: Black People Tell the Story of Reconstruction.* Garden City, N.Y.: Doubleday, 1976.

Tourgée, Albion Winegar. *The Invisible Empire*. New York: Fords, 1880.

Trelease, Allen W. *White Terror: The Ku Klux Klan Conspiracy and Southern Reconstruction*. Baton Rouge: Louisiana State University Press, 1995.

Williams, Kidada E. *They Left Great Marks on Me: African American Testimonies of Racial Violence from Emancipation to World War I*. New York: New York University Press, 2012.

Williams, Lou Falkner. *The Great South Carolina Ku Klux Klan Trials, 1871–1872*. Athens: University of Georgia Press, 1996.

Index